Read This or Die!

Read This or Die!

*Persuading Yourself
to a
Better Life*

RAY EDWARDS
with **JEFF GOINS**

HarperOne
An Imprint of HarperCollinsPublishers

HarperCollins books may be purchased for educational, business, or sales promotional use. For information, please email the Special Markets Department at SPsales@harpercollins.com.

FIRST EDITION

Library of Congress Cataloging-in-Publication Data is available upon request.

ISBN 978-0-06-307486-6

23 24 25 26 27 LBC 5 4 3 2 1

To my friend Robin Helton, who has preceded me in piercing that last and greatest of all mysteries.

Big ideas come from the unconscious. This is true in art, in science, and in advertising. But your unconscious has to be well informed, or your idea will be irrelevant. Stuff your conscious mind with information, then unhook your rational thought process.

—David Ogilvy, *Ogilvy on Advertising*

Contents

CONTENTS

Part V· Opportunity—The Invitation to Change

Part VI· Response—Making It Stick

Saved by a Sales Letter

 People are generally better persuaded by the reasons which they have themselves discovered than by those which have come into the mind of others.
——BLAISE PASCAL

IN MAY 2011, MY BODY began to rebel against my brain. At a business conference in Las Vegas, I was in the audience taking notes, having trouble keeping up with the speaker. My mind would think what I needed to write, but then my hand moved too slowly to get it down. *That's odd,* I thought. The person leading the seminar noticed I was having trouble and stopped presenting to ask from stage, "Are you okay?"

"Yeah," I said, distracted. "I'm just not feeling well."

This statement was true, but something else was happening, too—something that scared me. As I paid closer attention, I noticed my handwriting getting smaller and smaller, to the point of being practically illegible by the end of the day. When I returned to my room, I did some googling, and the number one result for my symptoms was Parkinson's disease. I sighed. Returning home, I called our family physician in Spokane to tell him my symptoms.

"Come in," he said. "Let's talk."

During our visit, my doctor said, "You're much too young to have Parkinson's disease, so I want you to stop being concerned about that. I'm certain that's not what it is. You're forty-five years old, Ray. That can't be what's happening."

I agreed with him, nodding, already feeling a small sense of relief.

"But to make you feel better," he continued, "I'll get you an appointment with a neurologist who can verify that, so we can figure out what's really going on. I think it's probably an impinged nerve in your shoulder."

It was months before I was able to see that neurologist; and though I left that initial appointment with my family doctor feeling better, my symptoms only continued to worsen.

Something was definitely wrong.

On September 22, 2011, the day before my forty-sixth birthday, my wife, Lynn, and I went to see the neurologist. I didn't know it at the time, but the doctor made a diagnosis within sixty seconds of seeing me. She knew the hallmark signs, and I had them all. After five minutes of examination, she said, "I think you have Parkinson's disease. This is serious. It is degenerative, which means it only gets worse. There's nothing we can do to treat it or make it better. It is eventually going to make you dependent on other people to do the most basic of tasks, like getting dressed and eating. You're going to have difficulty walking. You could be in a wheelchair or otherwise disabled in seven years. You have a limited window on your ability to function normally. There are medications you can take to treat the symptoms, but they only work for a little while, and they cause their own side effects that are problematic."

Lynn and I stared at the neurologist, stunned. Surely, we thought, there had to be another way. Devout Christians that we were, we considered the diagnosis a test of faith, a good setup for our new career as healing evangelists. Once I got healed, I'd be able to use such a testimony for the edification of others: teaching and preaching and healing, just like Jesus. My whole life, I'd prided myself on being a positive thinker, someone who could imagine a better future for himself and then create it. I believed in the power of prayer and physical healing, even modern-day miracles. I'd followed the self-help gurus for decades and taught their practices and philosophies in my own business. As an established copywriter, I thought you could convince anyone to believe anything. And here I was, sitting in a neurologist's office, unable to accept what she was telling me. *I was sick, and there was no getting better? Really?*

This, by the way, is the part of the grieving process they call *denial*.

The morning I experienced my first few shuddering tremors, a few months after that initial diagnosis, my coffee cup looked like one of those mud puddles in *Jurassic Park*, quaking with each unexpected vibration. A monster was, indeed, approaching. That was the first time I felt real, honest-to-God, gut-wrenching fear about what was to come. And as the reality of the diagnosis set in, I got scared—for myself, for my wife, for my family and employees and everyone who was depending on me. I wasn't ready to die and certainly didn't want to go this way, as a shaky invalid who can't control himself and is dependent on others. *It wasn't supposed to be this way,* I thought. *This isn't fair. What did I do to deserve this?* I don't have to tell you that none of these thoughts made my life one iota better, but I still thought them. Then, after a *long* period of wound-licking, catastrophizing, and reflecting, I turned to an ally I never would have considered. It wasn't faith healing or positive thinking that saved me. No, it was something far less conspicuous.

Writing.

I didn't write my Parkinson's away, but I used words to understand what I could and could not control. This was a long, difficult process. First, I questioned the diagnosis, trying to bargain with reality. I went for second and third opinions, looking for any "loophole" I could find and finding none. Then, I figured there must be a way out of this situation, some magic pill I could take to reverse the symptoms, a series of special words to recite that would convince God to heal this thing right out of my body. As an entrepreneur, I possessed the audacious belief that I could fix almost any problem, which served me well in many areas of life for many years. But now, that belief only served to make me angrier. I couldn't fix this, couldn't fix anything. I was stuck and didn't have any way out of a terrible situation. I was desperate. So I did something nobody would ever have expected.

I wrote myself a letter.

Words Change Everything

This is a book about change—the kind we hope for and the kind that sometimes comes unexpectedly and in unwelcome ways. When I received my Parkinson's diagnosis, I did not want my life to change. I wasn't looking for the kind of transformation that you seek at a weekend seminar, something dramatic and powerful to accelerate my evolution as a human being; and yet, that's just what I got. Life is funny that way. The things we don't want to happen, that we can't see coming, sometimes happen—no matter how hard we believe in their alternatives. This experience of acquiring an incurable illness brought me to an impasse in terms of my own beliefs and the way that I was used to living. My old way of looking at the world, the ideas on which I'd built an entire life for half a century, had been broken apart, and I wasn't sure what came next.

And this, my friend, is the starting place of every good story and every great ad.

I am considered an expert at professional copywriting. For the past four decades, I have taught people a process for convincing consumers why they need whatever the business is selling. I was trained in and then studied on my own the science of persuasion, methods for helping people change their minds and alter their decisions. Changing a person's mind, when you know how to do it, is relatively easy. It's not magic. All you have to do is help people convince themselves that what they want is within reach and then show them how to get it. This is all marketing is: identifying a problem in a person's life, amplifying the pain to the point of necessary action, and then providing the next right step. Anyone can do this if they understand the process. You really can change a person's life by changing their mind; and changing people's minds, by another name, is "sales." Sales is the art of helping someone see a product as *the* solution to their problem, so that it becomes their idea to buy it. Think of it as assisted decision-making: you're helping someone convince themselves that they need to buy this thing to relieve their discomfort and that, if they don't, it'll only hurt worse later.

Human beings tend to change only when they must, and the only one who can convince a person that change is necessary is themselves. A good salesperson, then, doesn't pressure or force someone to purchase something. Good salespeople blithely lead their prospects to a place where they are the ones convincing themselves that buying this product is necessary. We marketers and salespeople understand that people are much better at convincing themselves of something than we are. I got to that place after flailing around for a time, when I faced the very real prospect of my business failing and my wife being left with nothing but a depressed, ailing husband, and I realized I faced an impossible situation, one in which something *had to* change.

So I tried an experiment. If I couldn't change the circumstance itself, maybe I could change my mind about it—maybe I could change me. I knew that if anyone had a chance at persuading me that this was even possible, it would be me. How I persuaded myself to change despite desperate circumstances is what this book is about.

As a marketer and trainer persuader, I understand that persuasion is a delicate process and must be done right. When you persuade someone, you are creating urgency in them, so that they act *now*, instead of later. People are persuaded whenever they buy something, vote, or make even the tiniest of decisions. In small but significant ways, we all make decisions on a daily basis without even being conscious of it. Over my many years of studying this craft, I've realized there is a simple framework for understanding what it takes to change a person's mind. Sales starts with words, and copywriting is the art of using the right words to motivate people to make the desired changes in their lives.

Copywriting is an ancient craft, one that's been motivating people to make big changes for millennia. In ancient times, philosophers used words to debate how the universe worked, writing proofs to convince one another of their arguments. The *Ninety-Five*

Theses Martin Luther tacked on those cathedral doors was, in fact, a sales letter. The Declaration of Independence was a form of defiant persuasion, signaling to the king and the rest of the world that the loosely banded colonies would not tolerate tyranny. All change starts with words. And lest you need more examples, let's not forget *The Communist Manifesto*, *Mein Kampf*, and many others—all examples of how writing can stir people to do all kinds of things, whether for good or for evil. Words are powerful. So whether the purpose is religious, ideological, political, propagandistic, or just plain hateful, human beings have been using language to create change for a long time.

Granted, not all change is equal or even beneficial; the words we use, and how we use them, matter. To effectively persuade another person, you have to use the right words in the right way to convince the person that change is necessary. Of course, people pretend not to like change, but most love it. People change their minds and habits every day, albeit often in small and nearly unnoticeable ways. You can see these changes in your own life. Whenever you decide to buy a certain laundry detergent instead of your typical brand because of the "100 percent all-natural" sticker on the label, you are changing your mind. When you opt to go with your spouse's movie choice for date night instead of your own, you are allowing yourself to be persuaded (and are wiser for doing so!). Human beings love to change their minds; they just don't like having changes happen to them against their will—and that distinction is key. We all use persuasion to convince others and ourselves to make all kinds of changes each and every day. Thanks to my vocation, I see persuasion everywhere, and I happen to be pretty good at it myself. But somehow, in my forty years of persuading people for a living, I had never seriously turned the process on myself.

To be fair, I never really had a reason to do so.

When something completely unexpected and absolutely devastating occurs, however, that's when you need to bring out the big guns. The most important motivator in a person's life is pain, and when one of the worst things imaginable happens, you'll try just about anything. After a lot of kicking and screaming regarding my incurable condition, I eventually got sick of all the wallowing and wanted the best version of my life possible. Denial wasn't working. Positive thinking had failed, too. Even my religious convictions were holding on by a thread. I was desperate for a solution I could trust. That's when I turned to persuasion.

If I couldn't change my circumstances, I reasoned, maybe I could change my perspective on them. And that's how the process started: not with huge aspirations of "changing my life," but just with a simple desire to feel better. That's how it works. You don't need a slogan or flashy marketing campaign to change a life. You just need a hefty dose of reality, a little discontent with the way things are, and the possibility of something better. When people are sick and tired of being sick and tired, they're experiencing plenty of pain to motivate them to get out of whatever ruts they might be in. That's what happened to me. That's *all* that happened to me. Putting my powers of persuasion to work, I convinced myself that this really terrible situation was truly for my own good and that my greatest life was still possible.

You know what? My sales pitch worked. Turns out I'm a pretty good salesman. You're good at sales, too; you just don't know it yet.

The Letter That Saved Me

Here is the letter I wrote that changed the course of my life. The rest of the book will explain in more detail why I structured the letter this way, why it worked, and how you can write a similar letter and change your life. I should warn you that the letter is a little raw in places. Then again, I was writing only to myself.

Attention: Ray Edwards

READ THIS OR DIE!
If You Don't Change, You're Going to *Bleed* Regret

Dear Ray,
You've heard that saying, "You shall know the truth, and the truth shall set you free"? Well, the truth *will* set you free, but first it will *piss you off*.

Look, I get it. It's hard to accept the fact you've been making the same mistakes for decades . . . vowing over and over again that "this time" you "absolutely" were "a changed man." Hard to accept that you've been screwing up these things for forty-five years. The only thing that could be worse would be you letting it roll over to *forty-six* years.

Why Did You Wait Until Now?

Simple things you already knew:

1. Eat good food, get lots of exercise, and rest.
2. Spend less than you earn, invest the difference, and don't borrow money.
3. Don't sacrifice quality time with family and friends for accolades and "image."

But because you ignored the wise counsel of your grandmother, you are now

1. fat,
2. sick,
3. broke,
4. in debt, and
5. disgraced.

And when you look in the mirror, you know the fullness of the truth: **you've already burned up your second chances and your "Get Out of Jail Free" cards.** I mean, you're freakin' forty-five now. And you have Parkinson's. The "Old Man" already had his shaky foot in the door, and he's trying to push his way into the house so he can put up his feet and start making an even *bigger* mess of your so-called life.

Now it's life-or-death time. **Are you a good man or are you a lying loser?** Sure, you'd never put it that way to anyone *else*, but you know, in your heart, that it absolutely *is* that simple. *Here are the lions, crouched outside your door, waiting to see whether you will let them eat you alive . . .*

*   **Death.** Death at the end of neurodegenerative disease is not pretty, nor is it pleasant.
*   **Disability.** You think you've had some tough going so far in your forty-five years? Try dealing with all your same problems, and then imagine not being able to walk, talk, dress, or even feed yourself. When *that* day comes, what will be your excuse?
*   **Regret.** You may have a slim chance of fixing all the stuff you've screwed up . . . but the clock is ticking, my friend.

What will your wife think? What will your son think? And let's get real—what should they think?

Because we both know the truth, Sunshine. You had the chance, over and over again. God blessed you with so much—so much time, so many talents, gifts, and privileges. And you wasted most of it. You traded fleeting pleasures for the treasure of your life.

Is that the legacy you want to leave?

"But What Can I Do? It's Too Late Now!"

Oh, please. Stop being a drama queen. You know that if you live, you still have a chance to clean up the mess you've made. But maybe just *one chance*. You're at the place, Sonny Jim, where you get no more do-overs.

You know you can get your life in order. And you also know that until now, you simply haven't wanted it badly enough to just go and *do the hard work*.

Here's the truth: The success you seek is simple, but not easy. You already know what to do. Here's the only question: *Will you actually do it?*

Here's How It Could Look

You have the power to make the changes you need and turn around your finances, your health, and your relationships. You still have the power to alter your own destiny for the better—and to do the same for all those around you.

If you're willing to make the effort, your life could look like this in five to ten years:

1. You have a balanced routine of rest, work, and play.
2. You have all the money you need to take care of yourself and your family—even if you never do another day's work in your life.

3. You have the respect of your wife and son.

4. You're able to help all the people you want to help.

5. Your positive impact on the world will outlive you.

6. You can prolong the life of your remaining years, not just the years in your remaining life.

All it takes is for you to make a plan and stick to it. That's all. Just get up every day and do what's required for that day—whether you feel like it or not.

Are you up for the challenge?

What to Do Now

Cultivate these habits:

+ Eat two meals a day (TMAD) ketogenic diet every day: carbohydrates 5 percent (maximum 20 grams), protein 25 percent (94 grams), fat 70 percent (117 grams); calorie budget ≤ 1,500.

+ Exercise seven days a week (cardio every day, strength training three days a week, "active rest" one day a week).

+ Pray or meditate daily, two times each day, at least thirty minutes each session.

+ Work only five days per week, meetings only three days a week, never book more than 60 percent of hours.

Follow this twelve-point code of conduct:

1. I do my best to help other people at all times and to keep myself physically strong, mentally awake, and morally centered.

2. I act in a manner that is cheerful, polite, friendly, and courteous.

3. I take 100 percent ownership of my emotional state and my response to life.

4. I follow my current morning and evening success rituals consistently.

5. I progress daily toward the achievement of worthy goals.

6. I engage in physical exercise for one hour per day.

7. I eat food, not too much, mostly plants, no sugar or flour.

8. I don't drink alcohol or use other intoxicants to numb my feelings.

9. I commit to consistently being even more tolerant toward other people (and their faults, failings, and mistakes). I place the best possible interpretation on their actions.

10. I act as if successes are inevitable and I already am the sort of person God created me to be.

11. I will ignore and completely close my mind to all pessimistic and negative facts that I can do nothing to change. I will actively seek the positive outcomes such facts or circumstances make possible through the intentional management of my thoughts and actions.

12. *Personal creed:* Let me honor God in all things. Let me strive every moment of my life to make myself better, as the Lord empowers me, that all may prosper. Let me think of what is right and lend all my assistance to those who need it, with no regard for anything but justice. Let me take what comes with a smile, without loss of courage. Let me be considerate of my country, of my fellow citizens, and my associates in everything I say and do. Let me do right to all, and wrong to none.

Why We Don't Change

Many of us want to change our lives, but few do. You don't have to look far to see the evidence. Abraham Maslow estimated that only 1 to 2 percent of the population ever fully become self-actualized, which means that almost nobody becomes who they could be. Why, exactly, *is* that?

I think it's because we are so in love with the way we've chosen to see the world that we forget there was a time when we saw things differently. Not long ago, where you are standing now seemed completely out of reach. Why, then, do you consider some future desired change nearly impossible? We humans are great at remembering the past and projecting it into the future but quite terrible at imagining something dramatically different from what has been. I learned this the hard way, with suffering as my ever-present teacher, but I wrote this book so that your experience can be easier. In these pages, I share a process I've been using for years, which I never thought to apply directly on myself—until it became necessary. It turns out that the way I've been persuading people for decades isn't just a good recipe for convincing someone to buy a TV. It's also a pretty good tool for changing your life.

Most of us don't change our lives proactively. Instead, we wait for tumultuous events to rock us awake, shaking us into a state in which we have to change. We must. We are *compelled*. Does it have to be this way, though? Do we have to wait for our lives to get absolutely terrible before we are willing to quit our self-destructive patterns and find the freedom we yearn for? I am convinced that those who are best at changing their lives are not necessarily special. They have merely learned to apply this process in a more proactive way than the rest of us. They don't have to wait for things to get absolutely terrible before losing the weight, quitting the job, and making that big change. I don't say this from an ivory tower of knowledge and wisdom. I am one of the poor saps who learned the hard way—but maybe you don't have to be.

In this book, I want to make it easy for you. I believe everything you need to transform your life is available to you right now. You just need to learn to use the tools already at your disposal. Few people make these changes in their lives—not because they don't want to, but because they lack the understanding. How do you make these changes? With words. You sell yourself on what's possible by beginning with what's intolerable. You convince yourself that you need to change, and then you do. This is what advertising is all about: selling the one thing every human being wants, the one thing they think they need. And what *is* that? It depends on the person. What I will offer in this book is a road map to get you there faster, so that you can see for yourself. It doesn't have to take a long time to change your life, nor does something cataclysmic need to occur for you to get started. What does need to happen, however, is that you must feel that change is urgent and necessary. We can change our minds whenever we want. We can change our lives whenever we choose to do so. Something we thought would destroy us can end up being the best thing that ever happened to us—if we really want to change.

Still, we tend to resist this process, defaulting to pain and urgency as our chief motivators. The purpose of this book is to show you a better way, so things don't have to get quite so awful before you make a change. As you read my story and the lessons I learned along the way, I hope you can apply these principles to whatever situation you're facing—big or small. And I truly hope you don't have to face the same hardships I did, but if you do experience what I experienced (or something worse), know that these principles work in those situations, too.

When my world was rocked by the realization that Parkinson's disease was going to devastate my mind and body, the very fabric of my reality was tested. Multiple times, I sought healing and help. If I believed strongly enough, I thought, then *surely* I'd be able to get rid of this pesky illness. It didn't work out that way, though. I tried and tried, chasing itinerant healers and prayer services galore, attending countless rallies and seminars, even repenting of every hidden sin I could imagine. But none of it worked. It all just led me deeper into a pit of despair, wondering what was wrong with me and what there was left for me to try. Sometimes, however, trying harder isn't the answer. Sometimes, you need to find another way to the summit.

If the way you've been doing things hasn't been working, if there is deep pain in your life that just doesn't want to go away, maybe another way is possible. Maybe there's a better life waiting for you, one that you just can't see yet. Maybe it's time to start writing.

Your Beliefs Aren't Working

Right before you get to your best life yet, you have to face all the beliefs that created the one you're living now. As I was plumbing the depths of my own self-pity, I found myself grasping for anything that allowed me to make sense of my unfortunate situation. *Why had God done this to me? Had my faith failed? Was I being punished?* No answer satisfied, and in that place of deep frustration, I considered another path. I began to wonder; to question; to consider alternatives to the current reality, which was becoming a living hell for me. As bad as my Parkinson's was, the belief that *this was all my fault* hurt even worse. And as I examined my beliefs, I started to see them for what they were—immature ideas—and they began to dissipate.

When people talk about "letting go," I used to think they meant some noble and heroic shedding of a core piece of your identity. I thought this would require effort. Now, I understand the act of letting go to be quite natural, like trying to walk upstream for hours only to lie back and let your body float with the water. You don't do anything; in fact, you simply stop fighting the way things are. The Buddha said his teachings were like a boat, leading his disciples to a new land. The point of his teachings was that once you reached your destination, you had to get out of the boat. That's letting go. So when many of my beliefs about the way things *should be* failed, I began to let go of what was no longer true. Everything I had believed up to this point had served me, leading me to this moment; but now, it was time for something new. What, exactly? I didn't know, but I was curious. If I had been getting the "radio signal" wrong, perhaps I could tune the dial to a new station. Maybe I could find something deeper and truer.

My goal wasn't to get rid of anything; it was to go deeper, to investigate my own thoughts and beliefs and see where I might have gone wrong. I didn't know what was true, but I knew what wasn't working anymore. I was open and curious about what could be, which made me ripe for persuasion. When you sell things for a living, as I do, you don't need a prospective customer to know what they want. You just need someone with a problem, someone with a little pain or discomfort. That's where all persuasion starts, and that's what I had: a big steaming pile of problems. At least, that's how I saw my life at the time.

Everything I know about persuasion, I've learned from direct-response copywriting. You know the kind I'm talking about: long-form, old-school sales letters you might still get in the mail from an out-of-touch insurance company. It's the same thing you may see on an old web page—fake yellow highlighting, text circled in red, artificial signatures. I won't hide the fact that I love copywriting. It's so much more than the highlighting and red lines for which it is often lampooned. There is a lot more to direct-response sales than grandiose promises and 100 percent money-back guarantees. You can change the world with this stuff, and many people have. Having worked in this industry for years, writing sales letters for many of the world's top personal development leaders, I knew how to use the written word to convince anyone of almost anything. I wondered whether I could convince myself of the unimaginable: that if I didn't change my mind about Parkinson's, it was going to kill me.

To move people from unwilling passersby to active participants in anything, you have to help them see that the thing you're selling is precisely what they've been looking for—the key to their happiness, you might say, or their relief from whatever discomfort they're experiencing. I've seen firsthand that this process can work in ways that objectively improve the lives of others. I've also seen persuasion used to manipulate honest people into doing stupid things. What I know for sure is that this stuff works. Nothing persuades better than a little pain and the next right step. So, I thought audaciously, what could it hurt to try?

What happened next was—well, maybe not miraculous, but at the very least—*interesting*.

Change Starts with You

Our entire lives are based on what we believe, so what happens when you upend everything you thought was true? Your whole life changes, that's what. Of course, it's almost impossible to get a person to accept something new, unless you tell it to them in a way they want to hear. You can't change someone who doesn't want to be changed, at least not easily. But we all seek transformation of some sort. As humans, we want to keep growing into what we could become, what we *know* we are capable of. No one wants to turn down a potentially better life, least of all the person who is slipping into an ever-worsening state of paralysis. But we also love the status quo, so it takes a painful moment, or at least the perception of one, to wake a person up. That was where I was. My body was breaking, and my list of "fixes" that could save me had been exhausted. My beliefs were no longer working, and I knew it. *Now* what? I was fed up with how my life had been going and was ready for change. Granted, this took time, but I began to understand that my way of viewing the world wasn't all there was.

Reality had more to offer than I was willing to see.

One of the best pieces of advice I received during that time of struggle was from Frank Kern, a successful ad man and copywriter. I was telling him about the things I was working on, sharing some of my health challenges and financial difficulties, and I kept saying, "This is so freaking hard, man! I'm working so hard." I was scared and looking for validation from a friend and peer I admired. I was seeking comfort, and he gave me none of it.

"Well, hang on a second, Ray," he said. "I see what you're saying. But what if it were easy?"

I laughed and played along for a moment. "Yeah!" I said enthusiastically. "What *if* it were easy?"

"No, seriously! Just pretend. What would that be like?"

Notice that he didn't tell me to think this way. He didn't tell me that it was true. He simply asked me to consider it, to imagine the possibility of what *that* might be like. This is how good persuasion begins. We don't thrust a new belief on someone; we don't demand they change. They can't. How they act is a function of what they believe, and everyone believes in what works, until it doesn't. As I had been confessing my frustration and despair to a friend, a belief of mine—*that I was helpless*—surfaced. And in that place of tenderness and openness, my friend invited me into a place of possibility. Was that all that could be true? He wasn't asking me to commit to anything, just to wonder. And I did.

What *would* that be like? How would a person with my face and name and lack of head hair act under such circumstances? If I still had the same stuff to do, the same problems haunting me, but it were easy, what would I do then? My body felt a little lighter just at the thought of it. My mind began to expand. The thought *This is hard and I hate it* expanded into something far less cumbersome. "Well," I replied. "If it were easy, I'd just be like, 'Okay, that'll be fun.' I'd just show up. I'd do it. It might even be a good time."

Damnit, Kern! You got me again.

With the right motivation, I can believe almost anything—and so can you.

Persuading Yourself to a Better Life

Marketing is neither good nor bad; it is simply a way to motivate people. We all know such intentions can be used for noble or nefarious purposes. It doesn't hurt, then, to be aware of the tactics often used to persuade us. That way, at the very least, we won't fall victim to other people's agendas. I was always captivated by what it took to change a person, as I had benefited from the personal development gurus of the twentieth century myself. Over time, though, I went from studying persuasion to teaching it, devising my own approach to this process, called the PASTOR method.

Most people associate the term "pastor" with a preacher, but the original meaning of the word is "to shepherd." I always liked the comparison between nurturing an audience and caring for, feeding, and protecting a flock. PASTOR can also be a helpful acronym, and we marketers love acronyms. Whether you're persuading someone else or yourself, this is a process that will help a person change what they believe and have them thinking it was their idea.

In this book, we'll be exploring each of these topics, as they made up the very process I used to change my life. Here's the overview:

P: The pain you are addressing. All solutions begin with problems, and before things get better, we have to acknowledge how bad they really are. You don't sell a new product by simply telling people what it is; you have to begin with your would-be customers and what they want. And everyone wants a little relief, a little comfort for the pain of existence.

A: Amplify the pain. It's not enough for something to hurt before you are willing to change; things actually almost always have to get worse before they get better. In a twelve-step program, this is known as "hitting rock bottom." The power of amplification, however, is that you can go there in your mind before ever having to do so physically. The thought of going bankrupt, when fully felt as possible, can save you from actual financial ruin.

S: Start searching for the solution. The solution will ultimately be founded on a new set of beliefs in some form and will include a systematic way of deepening and following those beliefs. When my friend Frank told me to imagine the possibility of things being easy, the temptation to believe something else could be possible was all it took to begin the process of moving toward a better future.

T: Transformation. Why would we consider changing? The reason is that the pain that we have to go through is less than the pain of standing still, and transformation is the result of that process. It's the rock-hard abs we'd love to have, the perfect vacation getaway, the life we've always wanted. We have to not only see the possibility but understand exactly what we'll get before we're willing to endure discomfort for the sake of change.

O: Offer. This is the price you'll have to pay to get there—the price of success. Change your diet, your belief system, your exercise program. On a sales page, the offer is literally the section where we say, "This is how much it costs and exactly how to buy it." An easy way to increase conversions in a sales letter is to very clearly tell people what to do; they don't want to have to work hard to begin the process. That's why you'll see calls to action such as "Click here," "Get started," and "Begin today!" People want to know the first step is easy and accessible.

R: Require a response. You have to do it. You have to do what you're selling yourself on doing. This is the end point, where you respond to the offer; you understand the cost of waiting and of missing out. We all tend to avoid taking action until we are required to give a response, whether it's a countdown clock that gets us to act now or a limited-time bonus that pushes us over the edge. The same is true for any change you're trying to create. The best way to get your prospect to not procrastinate is to make the situation seem urgent.

This is a process that can convince a person to lose weight, join a new religion, or swing their vote. Changing someone's mind is a subtle craft, one that takes years to master, but it works. When I was personally bereft, I needed a new perspective. I needed to believe the words of my friend that this could be *easy*. I wanted to trust that it could be the best thing that had ever happened to me. But I couldn't. I'd lost hope and didn't know where to turn. Once you've dipped your toe into depression, it's hard to remove yourself from the mire of despair. I wanted to believe, but I had my doubts. I needed to be persuaded.

So I wrote myself a sales letter.

It wasn't until I got Parkinson's that it became apparent how bad my life had gotten, even before my diagnosis. I was overweight, edging toward bankruptcy, and pessimistic about life in general. C. S. Lewis wrote that God whispers to us in our pleasures and shouts to us in our pain. I'd been needing a change for quite some time and finally was getting the message.

For years, I'd been using the PASTOR method to help others change their lives. Now, it was time to take my own medicine. I acknowledged a problem I couldn't solve and began to persuade myself that something else was possible. When we want to change our lives, we must be willing to look at the possibility of another reality. *Imagine*, Frank had said. *Just consider it.*

In my experience, though, human beings are not willing to endure radical change just because they feel like a change. Often, transformation must be thrust upon us as something that *needs* to happen now. It must feel like a matter of life and death. How, then, do we change before we have to, before it's too late and we've wasted years wallowing in despair and regret? We have to sell ourselves. Persuasion is the process of tricking our brains into thinking a decision needs to happen now, even when it doesn't. That's how you grow faster than "the other guy," how you transform your circumstances before they destroy you, how you change before your life is over.

I want to share with you how I did this, how I'm still doing this, and how powerful this process can be. It saved my life. But to do this right, you can't just believe something new. You have to create a brand-new reality that you reinforce over and over again. In doing so, you reinvent yourself—or, more accurately, you refine yourself. When your beliefs stop working, you can follow a well-worn path to better beliefs, ones that will ultimately lead to a better life. And that path is persuasion.

This is a book about what to do when your most deeply held

ideals break, when everything you know falls apart, and you long for a better reality. This is a book about how to create the change in ourselves that we long for and at the same time doubt is possible. As you go through this process, changing yourself, you will then see how it is possible to help others do the same. But we're getting ahead of ourselves. My friend Frank gave me a challenge—*What if it were easy?*—and I took that to heart. Pulling my head out of my rear end, I opened my laptop and started typing a letter to myself.

As I always do, I started with a headline. In this case, it was: "Read this . . . or die!" This particular line was borrowed from the late, great Jim Rutz, who used it for a health product sales line. I figured if the line worked for the greatest copywriter ever, it might be good enough to save my life. At least, it was worth a try. Copywriting saved my life when just about everything else failed me, when I was on the verge of giving up myself. And it's not copywriting itself that is the magic, but the technology of language and belief that transformed my life from the inside out. Changing your life, as miraculous as it sounds, doesn't have to be a mysterious or complicated process. It can be as simple as choosing the right words to believe and believing them.

If you feel as though you've tried *everything* to create the change you want and just keep coming up empty, I can relate. That's where I was. And with absolute empathy, I'd like to offer you a challenge: Maybe it's time to take a different approach. Maybe it's time to stop trying to rearrange all the external details in your life so that you can be happy and instead go inward. Maybe it's time to change *you*. The magic of copywriting that I learned so many years ago was that the right words, when you believe them, can change just about anything. I am here today because I found the right words, and I believe the same kind of change is awaiting you, as well. All you need to do is find the right language to help you create the change you want. Before we get into all that, though, we have to start where every good copywriter begins: *with what hurts*.

DO THIS

Before we are ready to change, we have to feel enough pain to *want* to change. "Discomfort" won't do the trick—we are often uncomfortable, but not uncomfortable enough to make necessary changes that may hurt in the short term. What circumstance in your life is causing you enough pain to motivate you to make substantive changes? Write it down in a notebook or on a piece of paper, because we'll be revisiting that throughout this book.

PART I

Pain—Start with What Hurts

Before we can transform our situation, we must acknowledge the problem. All change begins with someone not getting what they want. We have to face reality, which includes owning up to the fact that life didn't work out the way we thought it would. Our delusions have failed us. Something isn't working; there is an obstacle standing between where we are and where we want to be. What's not working? The more accurately you can describe your problem, the deeper you will desire change and emotionally connect to it.

The way you describe your problem accurately is by asking the right questions. What I teach other copywriters is to first understand your audience. *Who are they? What's their world look like? What are their pains, their problems, their fears, their frustrations, their anxieties?* You have to do that for yourself, for your own problem. Who are you? What does your world look like? What are your pains, problems, fears, and frustrations? As the great copywriting legend Robert Collier once said, you have to "join the conversation that is already taking place in the reader's mind." What conversation is already taking place in your own mind? How can you use that conversation to motivate yourself to make some big moves?

When hoping for change, a good place to start is with what hurts. In the PASTOR method, *P* is for "pain." Follow the pain, and you'll find the cure.

Chapter 1

Letting Go of Lies We Love

 We must love them both, those whose opinions we share and those whose opinions we reject, for both have labored in the search for truth, and both have helped us in finding it.

—SAINT THOMAS AQUINAS

THIS IS A BOOK ABOUT changing your life by changing the way you see the world. With a mixture of time-tested strategies from the fields of psychology, direct-response marketing, and persuasion, I'll share what I've learned about how we can change our reality by altering our understanding of it. This process goes beyond cheap, self-help clichés; it gets right to the heart of what you believe about the world and how that affects everything. When we persuade others, we use evidence worth believing to convince another person that there is more to the world than what they are seeing. What I've learned is that you can do the same thing with yourself.

If you want to change your life, all you have to do is persuade yourself to see things differently. You have to change your beliefs. Doing so is not easy, of course, and most humans resist change of any kind, especially when it requires them to admit they were wrong. But changing beliefs is possible, and I would daresay necessary, if you want to live a fulfilling and honest life. We change our lives by questioning the beliefs that no longer work for us, adopting more useful ideas about the world, and then following a process that leads to true transformation.

This is the process I've taught people to use for years and finally started applying to my own life when things got really dark. Whether things are feeling dire or you could stand to tweak a few areas, the end result is the same. We are going to construct a more positive future than the one you can imagine. But first, we have to start at the beginning—how we ended up in whatever mess we find ourselves in.

Encountering the Unexplainable

It was April 2009. I shifted in my seat, massaging my fist into the small of my back, trying anything to alleviate the excruciating pain that shot across my back and down my leg. My wife and I were at Bethel Church in Redding, California, for a leadership conference. I had been dealing with this pain for a couple of weeks, and it was severe. If I turned to the left or right or tried to bend at the waist, it felt as though lightning was striking the base of my spine. The pain was so intense that it would make me gasp, falter, stumble, and stop dead in my tracks. I was taking 800 milligrams of ibuprofen every four hours, and this only managed to moderately dull the edge of the pain. But finally, one day during this conference, the incomparable preacher Bill Johnson was teaching. Bill is sort of the godfather of the modern charismatic Christian movement and is especially well-known in circles that deal in the miraculous. He is a gentle and loving man; I always enjoyed being around him.

"I want you all to stand and lay hands on the person in front of you," he said. "Pray for one another's physical ailments. This is a day of healing!" It all sounded good and spiritual, but I realized as I watched people pray for one another that a certain amount of cynicism had crept into my heart. I was jealous. I heard a voice in my mind say, "You need to learn to receive from people as if it were the first time," so I let the people around me know I was experiencing this excruciating back pain. A group of five or six laid hands on me and began to pray powerfully in deep faith that God would heal my back. Immediately, I felt a sensation of hot oil pouring down my spine. A little scared, I opened my eyes to look around and saw that no one had poured any such oil on me, but I had the sensation nonetheless. The group seemed to sense that something had happened, and they all stood back.

One gentleman said, "Well? Are you feeling anything?"

"I believe," I said quite calmly, almost sounding like Spock from *Star Trek*, "I have been healed."

Another man in the circle said, "Well, can you do something that you couldn't do before? Test it out."

I gingerly twisted my spine to the right and turned my torso a full ninety degrees in that direction. No pain. I then turned the same distance in the other direction. No pain. I began to bend over at the waist and rock back and forth, and suddenly I was celebrating, because the pain in my back was gone.

The next day, Lynn and I sat in the middle of a dimly lit room, bathed in blue stage light, swaying in a sea of bodies with hands raised and voices murmuring whispers and shouting to heaven. Some screamed "Hallelujah," and others knelt at the altar with anointing oil soaking their collars. I raised my hands in praise, the pain in my back gone, my faith on fire. The woman to my left stood with eyes closed, whispering in a language only few are privileged to speak and even fewer to understand. We were in the middle of a revival. We witnessed men, women, and children walk to the front, have hands laid on them, and be healed. It was amazing. I was seeing scenes from the Bible come alive before me.

"This is what we were born for," I said to my wife as I buckled my seat belt and turned the key in the ignition of our 2006 Holiday Rambler Admiral motorhome. "Heal full-time. Start a new life."

Lynn smiled and grabbed my hand, squeezing it. "I would like that," she said and buckled herself in.

Around this time, having just graduated from a ministry school, I received a phone call from a friend named Patrick.

"Ray," he said, "I've called to say goodbye." I asked what he meant, and he continued, "I've been diagnosed with stage 4 cancer. It has metastasized throughout my body. It's in every limb, every part of my body, and the doctor says that six months from now I will not be alive. He told me to put my affairs in order and to say my goodbyes, so that's why I'm calling you."

Having just seen many healings of smaller problems take place, I heard myself saying words that left my heart pounding: "I don't think that's the Lord's will for your life."

"What do you mean?" he asked.

"God didn't give you cancer, and he paid a price so you wouldn't have to have it, so I'd like to pray with you right now that Jesus would heal you completely of this disease. Is that okay with you?"

There was a brief silence, then he said, "Sure." I could hear in his voice an unspoken plea. "Don't you get my hopes up."

I prayed a very short prayer, something on the order of this: "Jesus, you paid the price. Let him be healed of this cancer now, in your name."

Then we went on to another topic of conversation and eventually hung up. He promised to let me know how he was doing. As I left the conversation, I was a little discouraged. I didn't feel a particular stirring of faith. The boldness of my words did not match what I felt inside, and I realized I'd only been going through the motions. I'd prayed what I thought I was supposed to pray, so if his healing was reliant on my faith, Patrick was in trouble.

I didn't hear from my friend for about six months and honestly more or less forgot about the conversation. One day, however, the phone rang, and there was his voice on the other end, vibrant and strong. "Ray," he said, excited, "I just got back from the oncologist, who laid two scans on the table in front of me and showed me in the one on the left how my body was filled with cancer. Then he showed me the scan on the right and said, 'Can you find the cancer in this scan?' I told him I could not. The doctor said, 'That's right, because it's not there.'" Patrick paused and then continued, "I sat there for a while and I finally said, 'How's that possible?' and the doctor said, 'Medically, it's not possible. I could only call this a miracle.'"

When Life Doesn't Turn Out the Way We Planned

My whole life, I've been a big dreamer. I've believed in miracles and the unknown; I've been a man of faith and inspired others to trust the unexplainable. By and large, this outlook on life has served me well. These beliefs guided me into maturity as an adult, gave me the tools I needed to trust myself as an entrepreneur, and even helped me navigate one of the hardest seasons of my life.

But there came a point when certain beliefs no longer helped me. In fact, they held me back. For some time, I thought belief itself was the problem; but the truth is that it was only my limited understanding of the truth, of what was real, that kept me from living my best life. Nonetheless, it took some time and persuading for me to be able to find a better version of my story, in which I had to surrender to how life was unfolding instead of trying to force the outcomes I wanted. To be honest, I'm still learning that lesson. I think it's one of the great lessons of our time here on Earth: life doesn't always work out the way you hope it will.

My plan was simple. I was going to live to 120 years old and stay in perfect health until the day I died. Through the power of positive thinking, with the right diet and three days a week of exercise plus a daily dose of supplements, I would live a long and healthy life. And if I got sick, God would heal me. It was all going to work out just fine. After all, I had seen and even experienced divine healings in church services, events that science could not explain. I was a true believer in so many things, the most ardent follower of some of the most outlandish principles.

And then came Parkinson's.

I was diagnosed with Parkinson's disease two years after I received the healing of my back at the revival service mentioned earlier. The first few months of my diagnosis, I was a moon-faced disciple, welcoming the brief sacrifice of my body for the inevitable glorification of God. I was to be healed. I knew I wasn't going to live forever, but "degeneration" wasn't part of the plan. So I waited for the healing to come. And I waited . . . and waited. And waited. Earnestly believing that Parkinson's would not last forever, in spite of the evidence, I *knew* there was something better waiting for me. This is the problem with a belief: it can guide you toward the change you want, but it can also hold you back from the life available to you now, as my belief was doing. Frustrated with my increasingly worsening condition, I attended all the healing events I could find. I discovered one such ministry in my own hometown, which was how I found myself standing in a rented hotel conference room, along with several hundred other people, all of us waiting to hear from a great healing evangelist.

The air was hot and sticky. The hotel staff had forgotten to turn on the air conditioner. The doors in the back were propped open to let more air in, and I periodically turned my face toward the open air to cool down. When I did so, I caught the eye of the woman behind me. "So what are you here for?" she asked, chewing gum between each word.

"I have Parkinson's disease," I told her.

"Stop," she said. "Stop that. Don't say that. Don't say you have Parkinson's. You don't have it."

"Well," I replied. "I do. I do have Parkinson's."

"No! You don't! You're just siding with the enemy."

Siding with the enemy? Hadn't that woman just asked me why I was there? Siding with the enemy was the last thing I wanted to do, but maybe she was right. I couldn't trust my own senses anymore. In my mind, I was following Jesus the best I knew how and doing everything I could to usher in a miracle. Still, this woman insisted what I was doing was wrong: "You're aligning yourself with the work of Satan. Don't ever let me hear you say that again. Every time you say it, you endorse the work of Satan in your life."

Oh, good. So I have that going for me now.

Blood ran red hot as it pounded through my arteries while a quickening pulse drummed staccato in my ears. I felt anger. Doubt. Fear. Confusion. *Was* it my fault that I continued to have Parkinson's? Even people in my own church family had echoed similar sentiments: "Don't confess, Ray! It comes from the devil. What you confess, you possess!" But just because something rhymes doesn't mean it's true. Does it?

A trusted friend told me over coffee one morning, "Look, I'm not judging you. I'm not saying you brought this on yourself or that somehow you're punishing yourself. But the more you acknowledge this disease, the longer you're going to have it."

Well, that's just BS, I thought. I had fought this thing tooth and nail from every angle I could conceive of, and still it stuck with me.

I was beginning to have my doubts—about healing, about God, about what was going to happen to me. Suddenly, I wasn't so sure that a healing was coming. My body was breaking, I was doing my best to fix it, and nothing was working. And all these opinions I was hearing from others were really starting to piss me off. Meanwhile, my business was struggling, and the money I was spending on treatment and chasing the latest healing craze was starting to make a real dent in our finances.

I was afraid to tell my wife about my doubts. Lynn was comforted by her faith, and I didn't want to destroy that. At the same time, I was facing a reality that challenged everything that used to be "true" for me. My old beliefs were conflicting with the way life seemed to be unfolding, and I desperately wanted to talk to my wife. I didn't want to cause more stress in our household, though, so I kept my thoughts to myself.

Our dinner table conversations consisted of pleasantries: "Hey, how are you doing?" "How was work?" There was nothing about my health, nothing about the dire state of our finances, nothing about how we both felt. She didn't want to know, and I didn't want to tell her. I felt like a failure, and her knowing would have made it all that much worse. Waffling between feeling like a victim and believing that change was still possible, I continued asking for healing, seeking out some unknown miracle, going to all the top names in the modern revivalist world. Each time there was a service, I went to the front, confessed whatever I could, and pleaded for relief. It never came.

Eventually, I stopped asking for prayer.

I didn't stop wanting to believe. But after dozens of people had told me I needed to go through some inner healing to reveal the "sins" that were causing me to be sick, there wasn't anything left to confess. Sure, I'm lustful. I can be gluttonous. Sometimes, I'm lazy. What more do you want? Oh, and sometimes I don't put the toilet seat up when I go pee, but a little dribble never hurt anybody. I wasn't hiding anything, and the healing wasn't coming. Apparently, sin wasn't my problem. So what was?

Staying positive wasn't working, either. I would think thoughts such as *Every day in every way, I'm getting better and better,* but that statement wasn't true anymore. It was a lie. In the past, if I had believed something strongly enough and repeated it enough times, it would often come true, or so it seemed. As a middle-aged white man in America, that prosperity formula worked for me—that is, until the irresistible force of my beliefs met the immovable object of a disease that would not be wished away.

Belief, meet reality. The two of you should talk.

Parkinson's is a neurological disorder that is degenerative and incurable. Every day was a struggle, and I was *not* getting better. The situation was getting worse and worse, and telling myself the opposite wasn't helping. Some believe that if you just stay positive about your life, then everything will work out. I used to be one of those people. But holding fast to a belief that contradicts reality is crazy-making. You end up gaslighting yourself, doubting your own perception and senses. This is corrosive to your integrity and no way to live. If you can't trust yourself, why would anyone else? And if you cannot trust how things seem to be, what can you trust? In times of crisis, we often fall back on our beliefs, those models for reality that fill in the gaps between what is known and unknown. And that's just what I did, until those very beliefs fell apart all around me, and

READ THIS OR DIE!

all that was left was whatever this was—this life I had to live that did not align with my expectations, dreams, or even wishes.

Even at that point, letting go of my old beliefs was a gradual process. Reality began to set in when my doctor told me, "You're not going to get better from this. You're going to die with this disease. You may not die *from* it, but you will die *with* it, and it will degrade the quality of your life from this day forward."

After hearing such dire news, I still held out hope for a while, but then hope started to hurt too much. The idea of a better life later, some magical healing in the future, eroded the possibility of a good life now. My hope was destroying what I was currently left with—which was this disease that did not want to go away. I had to learn with it, to integrate it into my life as well as I possibly could. But that's not where I was at this time. I was bereft. All my plans had failed. If I wasn't getting better, then I wasn't getting healed. And if I wasn't getting healed, I wouldn't be a healer. I would be something else: sinner, atheist, victim—and most assuredly *dead*. My beliefs had effectively been broken.

The Danger of Belief

Some say it doesn't matter what you believe, so long as you believe in *something*. I disagree. There is nothing so dangerous as a belief, especially a devout one, that is not grounded in reality. The world is riddled with terrorists and martyrs who do all kinds of things based on the sincerity of their beliefs. Depending on whom you ask, they may even be the same people. After all, one culture's terrorist is another's martyr; in the words of Oscar Wilde, "a thing is not necessarily true because a man is willing to die for it." In my case, I was willing to die for the possibility that God would heal me—until I wasn't. The belief that I would be healed was keeping me from the medicine my body needed, and I started to see the absurdity of that situation. Only a few months into my diagnosis, I was having trouble pushing the buttons through the loops in my shirt. I couldn't hold my hand steady enough to not bruise my gums while brushing my teeth. A bad belief can make everything in your life worse.

From 2013 to 2016, I poured myself into building my business. I was focused as never before on growing our revenues. We began having really successful product launches, had our first multi-six-figure launch for a copywriting program, and shortly thereafter started having seven-figure launches. My company would earn nearly a million dollars in a week or two. It was incredible. At the same time, my symptoms were getting worse, and no matter how much money I made, I couldn't seem to hold on to any of it. My life was falling apart, and I was in denial about the whole thing.

In 2016, I was traveling a lot for conferences and speaking engagements. One night while alone in a hotel room, as my Parkinson's symptoms were really starting to set in, I couldn't even walk across the room. From pain and neurological issues, my body was breaking down. Episodes like this one happened more and more at night, when my symptoms were always worse. As each day wore on, my energy levels would drop, and I would not be able to see other people as often. I felt too embarrassed, sometimes needing to disappear for weeks on end in an attempt to hide my symptoms from friends. My family knew, but not a lot of others understood what I was going through. I thought if my clients and colleagues knew, it would be the end of my career.

Everyday tasks such as handling a fork and knife were sometimes too difficult; I looked like a child trying to learn how to eat properly. When I walked, sometimes I looked as if I was drunk. So when I was away for events, I always tried to get back to my hotel room before those sorts of symptoms got worse. Once, around that time at a marketing conference, I had been out to dinner and had one drink of alcohol with my meal. Later, I had to be assisted to the curb to catch a cab. As people were walking out of the restaurant, they saw me and tried to talk to me, but as evening was approaching, I was already slurring my words. I was weaving in and out and had to have help to stand up. Someone chuckled and said, "Maybe a few too many tonight, huh, Edwards?" Everyone laughed, and I laughed, too, because what else could I do? It was humiliating.

No one knew about my disease at that point. I was still too afraid to tell the truth. But the alternative—being mistaken for a drunk—was hurtful. I wanted to explain: "No! You've got it all wrong!" But I knew I would not make a convincing advocate for myself in that moment, speech slurring, struggling to stand. At another event, I was walking down the hallway, holding on to the wall to keep from falling over, and I overheard someone laugh as they told their companion, "Someone's been hitting the bar early!" They didn't know that I could hear them. They probably never thought about it again, but I still feel hot when I think of the humiliation.

Other times, I found myself lying on the floor of the hotel suite, wondering how I would be able to get to the bathroom before my medicine took effect. That happened enough times that I finally realized it probably wasn't a good idea for me to be traveling alone anymore. I started paying for flight, hotel, meals, and all expenses for a team member and a caregiver to help me with physical needs. The expenses increased, and my stress levels went up, too, even though I had more help. My doctor kept telling me that what I needed was less stress, but I would tell him, "I need more money to have less stress." And to get more money, I had more stress. It was a vicious cycle. I wanted to do everything I could to keep up with the hype I was generating for myself in the marketplace—and not only that, but to generate enough income to cover payroll, which had ballooned to an unbelievable size. I was super generous with my staff, perhaps too generous; the quality of their work did not always match their pay. This was stressful, too. I wasn't sure how to keep growing my company, keep up with the strain of the work, and also pay attention to my health. Things had gotten bad enough that I knew I needed to change something, or quite frankly, I was going to kill myself.

Resisting What Is

The Buddha taught us that any kind of "attachment," any desire that things should be different from how they are, is going to lead to suffering. I had never wanted Parkinson's, had never dreamed of such a thing happening to me, and hated that it had happened. But more painful than the disease was the idea that things should be different, that I should be healed or think more positive thoughts. It's not a sin to hope for a miracle, but when what you think *should be* has no basis in reality, you're going to suffer. Conversely, when we release our expectations and allow reality to be whatever it is, we open ourselves up to a whole new experience of life that can be quite meaningful and joyful. This is what has happened to me since that fateful diagnosis. When I began to reshape my beliefs— that is, how I navigated my way through this maze called life—and began to accept the way things seemed to be, I started experiencing peace.

When we cannot live the life we want, we must accept the one we have. The sign of a mature person, I think, is not that they believe the same things their whole lives. Rather, people who are maturing and growing into better versions of themselves are constantly evaluating what they believe. So after a year or so of meeting every big-shot wailing evangelist I could find—and I'm pretty good at manipulating my way to the top of the pyramid—I realized, *This is not going to work for me.* I needed to figure out something else. I told my wife, "Look. This is not working for me. I can't go on contending for the breakthrough. I can't be on my knees any more than I've already been. It's time for me to get up and do something else. I'm going to try actual medicine."

I needed beliefs that would serve me better and that were consistent with what I knew to be true. Staying within my old faith-based system had led to my feeling guilty, ashamed, and isolated. That was true for me and many others I've met through this process. Now, hear me out: If it works for you—if you get cancer, someone prays for you, and you're instantly healed—then run with that. That's great; I'm a fan, even to this day. Such healing still happens, it's still glorious, and it's still a mystery. But it just didn't seem that it was likely to be my experience. And after so many attempts at trying to make healing work, I had to let go; it just wasn't working for me. As Byron Katie says, "When you argue with reality, you lose—but only 100 percent of the time." But what is reality? To think that we, at any point in time, have a 100 percent accurate view of what's happening is a delusion. If you pay attention, you will find out pretty quickly when you get off track, or rather when your belief system is no longer guiding you well. To insist that your map is still correct, in spite of the evidence pointing to the contrary—well, that'll lead to driving right off a cliff.

When you face the truth, whatever it is, the monster you fear is almost always smaller than you think. When you're afraid of something but don't know what it is, you must muster the courage to look it in the face and acknowledge it. That's a hard place to be, I know. As Friedrich Nietzsche once remarked, when you stare into the abyss, you may find it staring right back at you. That remark may mean a lot of different things, but at the very least, it seems to mean that some caves are darker than others and may contain more than a single dragon. So be careful. This is not a gentle journey. It can be a frightening realization to come to grips with your own inadequacy; and yet, until you do, nothing changes.

Once upon a time, I thought buying things would make me happy. I thought having credit cards was a way to get happier faster, because you could get more things sooner. So I would buy something new, it would feel good for a minute, then I'd go back to "normal," needing a slightly more intense experience next time. I would travel to a new place and feel good for a few days, then start fantasizing about my next trip. I thought this was happiness, or at least the closest I could get to it. And for a while, buying things felt good, but it didn't take long after clicking the purchase button for me to feel my happiness fading. Each time I bought something, the window of joy seemed to shorten. Whatever fulfillment I was getting out of being a spendthrift wasn't sustainable. Each time, it became harder and harder to reconcile what I believed would happen ("Being able to buy things I want will make me happy") and what actually happened ("I am stressed about my increasing lack of money"). Facing the truth hurts, but it stings the way an alcohol swab on a cut stings—because that's how healing happens. We've got to clean the wound before it can fully heal; or in our case, we have to acknowledge *what is* before we can attempt to change it.

My Parkinson's diagnosis made me realize my death was far closer than I'd thought, so I figured I had better make the most of my life—which meant facing up to some difficult realities. First, I had to deal with all this crap I'd accumulated along the way. I had to face the overwhelming debt I had collected over the years. I had to face my own irresponsibility and the consequences of my actions. And I had to face the disease and what it ultimately meant for me. This is true of every experience and certainly of every traumatic illness, injury, or difficult situation. At a certain point, we have to face it all—not just the experience, however traumatic, but also the reality that one day we will not be here. Your own mortality is the greatest gift you get from this life. Acknowledging your own imper-manence makes living that more valuable and therefore richer. No matter how painful or hard such a realization may be, we cannot change things until we first accept them.

When I was diagnosed with Parkinson's, I was forced to face my own death. I had to come to grips with the fact that I was mortal, that I was not going to get better over time, and that I would slowly (or maybe even quickly) deteriorate into dust. "Think of this as a sped-up aging process," my doctor told me—which, you know, didn't sound great. But that wasn't the only thing I had to reckon with: I also had to face $500,000 in debt, a marriage that was on cruise control, and a deep sense of unhappiness in almost every area of life. This is what it feels like to look at the truth of your existence. There's always a point at which you look at reality and say, "Well, everyone dies." No one has been able to think themselves into immortality, not on this planet. So at some point, for all of us, our physical bodies fall apart, malfunction, and cease to be. We die. You can believe you're going to live forever in this physical body, but you'll find that to be an increasingly disappointing pursuit. Optimism is not believing the best will always happen. It's making the best of what does happen.

When your beliefs break, the first thing you may notice is how surprised you are, how off-center you feel. *This isn't how the world is supposed to work, is it? And yet, here we are; apparently, there are some things you don't know and have been wrong about.* This stings; it is the feeling of growing up. Maturing is reconciling the way you thought things were with the way they actually are. We all have to grow up at some point, or we risk a lifetime of a Peter Pan fantasy, which is no life at all. Once you are properly disabused of your own distorted ways of seeing the world, you are free to see it as it is—and then, quite possibly, to change it.

DO THIS

Make a list of ideas, beliefs, and behaviors you know to be either outright false or detrimental to your health. This is for no one else to see but you. Be honest with yourself. No one else will read this, and you are not agreeing to change anything yet, just looking for those things that you know have not been working for you on some level.

Chapter 2

Facing Reality

 We do not see things as they are, we see them as we are.
—ANAÏS NIN

THERE IS A TIME IN life when easy explanations work, and it's called childhood. Simple answers can be helpful when one is a novice at a new endeavor who needs to understand the basics of something before getting sophisticated. If you knew how complex and scary any undertaking was, you might never get started! This is why self-help clichés *work*: they represent a truth behind what motivates people, which is that things ought to be simple. I don't begrudge easy answers, but maturity means the willingness to walk away from what we thought we knew—even if it requires an admission that we were wrong.

In my own experience of changing my life, I had to dismantle my beliefs about God, divine healing, church, and many other things. I had to find better beliefs that would help me see another way was possible. Otherwise, the alternative wasn't pretty. Maybe I didn't need to throw out the baby, but I at least needed to change the bathwater, because the baby kept pooping in it.

When we endeavor to change our lives, we have to begin with belief, with how we see the world. How does our current perspective align with or conflict with reality? Does our perspective help us more effectively make our way in the world, or does it cause unnecessary dissonance? What would we need to believe to create the kind of reality we want to live in? And is such a thing even possible? Indeed it is, if we understand what we're working with. You can't let go of a belief without replacing it with another. But doing so isn't as easy as it might sound.

Before You Can Change Reality, You Have to Face It

Where do beliefs come from? Think of something you believe and try to trace where it came from. It's hard, isn't it? That's because beliefs are unconscious. For many of us, our beliefs are foisted upon us, drilled into us by parents and pastors and politicians; some are taught by teachers, and others gained through experience. But what is a belief? A belief is a thought you feel strongly to be true.

But is it? *True*, I mean. A belief, I would argue, is neither true nor untrue. It is an idea, a thought you have an emotional attachment to; and just as emotions shift from sad to happy to angry, sometimes in a single moment, beliefs change, too. We don't always recognize this change when it's happening, and sometimes we hold on to old beliefs far past their expiration dates, but a belief is an abstraction of experience. Thinking of a belief as completely true or untrue is, quite frankly, not all that helpful. Are thoughts true? No, they are just ideas in your mind, some of which you can't even control.

So, to begin, when it comes to understanding how our brains process experience and turn our thoughts into beliefs, we need to identify all the influences that play into the human experience. First, let's look at reality.

Reality. This is the external world that cannot be argued with. I'm standing on the ground. The sun is shining. The wind is blowing. These things are reality, at least insofar as we can observe and perceive reality. Granted, if you want to get super philosophical, we could argue there's no way to know for sure that we all aren't just brains in a jar imagining this whole experience (that's a topic for another book, but if you want to get real nerdy, go ahead and google "solipsism" for an afternoon filled with fun).

Most of us living on planet Earth take certain things for granted. We don't argue about what we can perceive on a daily basis. We call this reality. It is the sun shining, the wind blowing, the child crying in the distance. Is it possible these are all just imagined phenomena, happening in our brains, some elaborate scheme to make us believe *The Matrix* is real? Sure. But to most of us, these are just facts; we don't need to argue about them. What we do with these facts, however, matters a great deal. Let's imagine, for instance, I encounter something in reality that causes a belief. I encounter the wind blowing and have a thought that I think is true. This is a belief. Because the wind is blowing a certain way and maybe I perceive the temperature to drop ever so slightly, I now believe a storm is coming. Maybe, I think, there's going to be a tornado soon, or spring weather is on its way. All these thoughts are not reality; they're my interpretation of reality. They are sentences in my head I feel certain are true. They're beliefs. Based on our definition of reality, they are not true in any perceivable way. They're just thoughts, ideas, concepts, which may or may not be true. They are our interpretations of reality, and these can be valuable and useful;

but they can also be misleading. Following our beliefs are what we call emotions.

Emotions. That thought, that sentence, that belief in my head about the weather, whatever it might be, sets off a storm of chemicals in my brain that are then released into the body. Neurotransmitters such as dopamine, serotonin, and norepinephrine are released and cause a vibration of energy, a sensation in the body. We call these emotions, or feelings, because we can actually feel them. When you're sad, if you pay close enough attention, you may notice a droopiness in your face; maybe you even want to cry. When you're happy, you may sense a warmth in the belly or chest. When you're angry, your face may get tense, and your chest may tighten. Embarrassment or shame can bring about discomfort in the stomach—and so on. Emotions are actual chemicals moving around in the body, and they are caused by thoughts that you think are true. These sensations in the body, these emotions—or "energy in motion," as they are sometimes called—cause behavior.

Behavior. What we feel, whether we realize it or not, causes us to act in a certain way. Of course, we may understand that anger can lead to violence or that loneliness may lead to a bout of drinking or texting an ex; but think about how difficult it is to concentrate when you're feeling frustrated or perhaps deeply in love. Emotions affect behavior, and many behaviors come from emotion. Think about it. When you feel great—happy, joyful, on top of the world—do you behave differently from when you feel dejected, sad, or depressed? Of course you do. Your behavior is controlled by feelings, and those feelings are driven by beliefs. Sometimes we can override these feelings with the rational mind, but that only lasts for a short time. We may end up suppressing our feelings, which will simply come out in other ways, perhaps in the form of an addiction or even physical illness. This is the reason it's so difficult to stop eating cake or drinking alcohol once it's become a habit, because let's face it—that stuff feels good. Why would we stop when we feel the pleasure of eating the cake or drinking the alcohol much more than we feel the logic of why it's bad for us? Feelings drive behavior—not always, but more often than we realize—which brings us to consequences.

Consequences. What we do results in what we experience. Our internal environment influences the external environment, and then the cycle starts all over again. Say, for example, that we got drunk or didn't get drunk, or that we went and worked out at the gym (or didn't). Each of these behaviors has a different outcome or result, which makes us feel differently, which in turn leads to our having a different thought, and on and on it goes. What we feel affects what we do, which produces a new environment that is then going to influence how we feel and think. But if we go through this process enough times, we will notice that the environments in which we find ourselves sometimes conflict with our beliefs about the world. This is called the gap.

The Gap. This is the moment of reflection after we see the consequences of our actions and decide whether or not we want to negate our reasons for doing what we've done or reinforce them. So let's say you did get drunk, which you thought was a good idea at the time, and now the next day you have a hangover and feel terrible. This gap is where you get to decide what you believe about the experience of getting drunk. Was it worth it? Was it a terrible idea? Do you have a drinking problem? Look, no judgment here. I enjoy a glass of bourbon more than most. All I'm saying is that every experience is an invitation to choose to keep believing whatever you believe or to change.

Beliefs are how we tend to navigate the gap, and they can be quite useful, necessary to survival, in fact. But, as Socrates taught us so long ago, the unexamined life is not worth living. I would amend that to say the unexamined belief may not be worth believing. Beliefs aren't true in themselves, but rather represent what we think is true.

So, how do you know when a belief is not working? Who's to say, exactly? Well, you. You are the ultimate arbiter of whether your beliefs are working or not. A good sign that a belief is broken is that it no longer aligns with reality. The gap between what *is* and what *you think should be* is so wide that it no longer makes sense to hold your belief anymore. It may be that this belief at some point was useful to you, something you thought was universally true; still, it may be time to let it go.

The Truth About Reality

I have found that reality never quite looks the way I want it to. I have also learned, in these many years of trying to resist what is, that I can't run away from belief. I can't divorce myself, even if I wanted to, from faith, because life is a gamble filled with mystery. There's so much we don't know, and the only way to navigate these confusing roads is to fill in the gaps between what we want to know and what we are able to know. In other words, I am still figuring this out.

Everyone believes something. This is not a choice; it is our nature to create constructs around human experience that help us make sense of the world. The world, as Frederick Buechner wrote, is a place where "beautiful and terrible things will happen." It can be pretty confusing, so we have to offer explanations for all this paradox, all this mystery. This is where belief comes in. There is nothing wrong with belief. If, in this book, I've somehow convinced you to drop your beliefs entirely, then I've failed. We can't not believe; furthermore, if we could stop believing, I wouldn't recommend doing so. Beliefs are necessary to living a deep and meaningful life. But for so long, I believed things that weren't working for me. And in that sense, my beliefs weren't true; they didn't help me get where I was going. Like an old GPS or an outdated operating system, a bad belief can do more harm than good.

What we believe can be an engine for change in our life. But a belief can also be a way of staying stuck wherever we are, doubling down on an old worldview that just isn't working. When your beliefs aren't working, it's time to put them to work. Test them, examine them, and consider which ones are worth holding on to and which ones need to be dropped or evolved.

Our experience of the world is based largely on what we believe—and, of course, our beliefs inform and create new experiences. For me, the idea that my disease was curable and I must be harboring some secret sin that prevented me from returning to good health was hurting me more than it was helping me. I slowly began peeling away the ideas I had come to take for granted as "truth." In fact, I tore many of them all the way down to the ground. Over time, what emerged from the existential rubble was a new construct, a new way of understanding reality. It wasn't the "Truth," with a capital T, some great answer upon which I could now base my entire life—at least not in the way I was used to thinking about such things. I didn't replace one belief system with another; rather, I discovered a newfound faith in *faith*, a belief that believing in something is better than believing in nothing. But for a belief to work, it has to align with your life as you are living it.

Perhaps that sounds a bit utilitarian, but I see no other way. Like scientists, we are constantly grappling with this experiment called life, trying out new theories and testing them to see what is useful. It is one thing to discover something as monumental as gravity and another to figure out how it works. Beliefs can be the same way. We may stumble upon something that seems true—a belief in God or science or an adherence to a certain moral code—but that doesn't mean we know everything about this thing. It doesn't mean we can't keep growing in our understanding. Like anything else, a belief can evolve and even be improved upon. This is how we get closer to what is real; we hold our ideologies loosely and replace the bad beliefs with better ones.

For a long time, I was delusional, continuing to hold on to belief systems that were no longer useful for me. In spite of my many attempts to pray and wish and declare it away, I still have Parkinson's— and believing that this was some necessary punishment for an unknown sin was simply too much for one person to bear. I realized the problem, though, wasn't reality; it was my understanding of it. My beliefs. If you're going to believe something, you might as well choose beliefs that work for you and help you, in some way, to live a better life. When you can't wish away the pain (and trust me, I've tried), the best you can do is to find a belief system that infuses suffering and confusion with meaning and purpose.

Testing What You Think You Know

What is it you want to change in your life? And how can you construct a new, positive bias around what you want to be true? You can collect evidence contrary to your belief. For example, you can replace "I'll never get married" with finding stories of people who are happily married and didn't find each other until later in life. Or, if your belief is "No one likes me," what evidence to the contrary could you look for? Scully and Mulder were right: the truth is out there. But it's far more malleable than we realize.

I'm always willing to adjust my conclusions based on new evidence. "Strong convictions, loosely held" is my motto—a powerful distinction from "I believe it just because I believe it." This motto has made a world of difference. This doesn't mean I'm looking for evidence to believe things that are clearly and patently untrue. But "true" and "useful" aren't necessarily the same. It is possible for something to be true and useless, and false and useful. Our goal in this process is to create the most useful beliefs possible that do not conflict with reality, as we currently understand it.

To change a belief, we have to change our thoughts; and this is hard. It takes practice and intentionality. We can, however, change what we think and believe by constantly reinforcing our new beliefs with evidence that shows what we believe is both accurate and useful. Which, of course, makes something easier to adopt.

Beliefs either work or don't work. How do you know whether a belief is useful? You have to test it. I had a system I was holding on to, and it wasn't working for me. Was it true? I don't know. All I know is that it wasn't useful. It just wasn't working, and that was enough reason to change it. If you want to believe that Martians live in your bathroom, that's fine. Start there. Believe that, but then test the belief. We can't dogmatically take any belief off the table and remain intellectually honest. We have to experiment.

To determine whether something is useful, we need to run it through the scientific method and see what it produces. Start with a hypothesis, look for evidence to prove it's true, and record your results. Pressure test the thing and see if it stands. You'll learn as you go. If you test a belief, however, and it doesn't hold up to this scrutiny, then it's a bad belief and worth reconsidering if not altogether dropping.

In my case, I started reading more about the science of my incurable condition. I had always been interested in understanding the way things work. Why is anything the way it is? Whether it's through science, art, or religion, we are all trying to figure out what life is about. With my Parkinson's, after my understanding of "faith" failed me, I went straight to science, reading as much material on the disease as I could. If I couldn't get better, I wanted to learn to manage my condition, maybe even lengthen my life—or at least minimize the pain.

The Science of Belief

One "catechism" that really sank deep in me and has stuck with me all these years is the scientific method. The process of having a hypothesis about why things are the way they are, testing that hypothesis, and then looking at the results and adjusting the theory seemed reliable and now more relevant than ever. As I navigated my own diagnosis and what it meant for me, I wanted to be open to a new process of understanding reality, one that might make things better instead of worse. So I returned to my age-old love affair with science. Science doesn't lie. It doesn't let you down. It doesn't pretend to know things that it has no business pontificating about—at least when we are truly following the scientific process and not just trying to sell our own propaganda.

At that time in my life—broke, lonely, and apparently speeding toward the grave—I started feeling like a victim. *Why me? What did I do? How come no one could fix this, especially me?* There was even a point at which I believed I'd be better off dead and that maybe everyone else's lives would be better off if I were no longer around. But I was only hiding; the shame of my own inability to cure myself and the judgment of others caused me to retreat from the world, both emotionally and physically. I didn't want others to know my life was such a mess. I felt that if people knew what was going on with me, particularly when it came to my finances, they would think, *How could you be so irresponsible? How could you be such a liar?* I was teaching people how to make money online, but I was spending more than I was making. My integrity was broken, and that was weighing on me.

It's a scary thing to face your own ineptitude, your own indulgence, your carelessness and ignorance and, well, your own humanity. To admit vulnerability is to put ourselves at risk; others could take this information and hurt us, after all. But what good is it to be loved by people who don't actually know you? This was what I began to understand: that as I was hiding significant parts of myself, life didn't feel worth living anymore.

I was fascinated by what I learned of the scientific method and how it proved to be a useful tool for belief. Ever since I was a boy, I had believed in God, but I had also loved science. I believed in the divine but watched *Star Trek*—which is another way of saying I was not cool. Mr. Spock, my favorite character, was all logic. I thought, *What a beautiful way for God to set up the world.* We can see evidence and come up with hypotheses about how something works. We can figure out how to test ideas to see whether they are true. And if an idea is true, I should be able to replicate that test time after time and get the same result. Then that idea becomes my theory.

A scientific theory can never be proved or disproved. That's the part of the scientific method that has most appealed to me over the years. It's like a way of saying to myself, "Okay, I don't have to be 100 percent right. I just have to get close to being right." What a relief! That said, applying the scientific method to belief is not the same thing as digging into a grab bag of ideologies, picking the beliefs you most fancy in any particular moment. Maybe that works for some people, but my analytical mind wanted something more substantive.

When testing a scientific theory, I knew you always had to begin with a question that led to research, allowing you to then construct a hypothesis. This seemed like the right way to figure things out. What was true? I didn't know, but I wondered whether I could employ such a system for understanding my own shifting ideas and doubts about this thing called reality. To remind you of a topic you may not have read about since high school, the steps of the scientific method are as follows:

1. Ask a question.
2. Do the research.
3. Form a hypothesis.
4. Conduct an experiment in which you test your hypothesis.
5. Collect and analyze as much data as you can from the experiment.
6. Draw a conclusion.
7. Communicate, share your results, and replicate.

Notice that last part of step 7: you replicate the process. In other words, it never ends; you just keep repeating the process with more information, hopefully drawing deeper and more accurate conclusions. In science, you do not worry about "Truth" in some cosmic sense of the word. You worry about what you can prove, what can be demonstrated and observed in real time, understanding that what you know is always evolving. And what we might call, in another area of life, belief or faith, we would call in science a hypothesis.

I undertook this process when I began exploring a more scientific means of dealing with my disease, going through clinical trials and trying out electromagnetic stimulation therapy for my frontal cortex. I'm hesitant to try anything that doesn't have at least some amount of data behind it, but I was also desperate. It was helpful to be willing to look at any particular hypothesis or theory without prejudice before walking all the way through it. How else would I know if it was right or not? I felt as though I was in the place of one of my favorite quotes by Richard Feynman: "The first principle is that you must not fool yourself—and you are the easiest to fool."

I appreciated that Einstein, with his theory of relativity, seemed to be saying that if you're going to believe something, you might as well make it good. Even if the model isn't completely accurate, you need a model. And who wants to believe in a bunch of nothingness? I don't.

But sometimes, the belief systems that have gotten us to where we are can't lead us through the next crisis or help achieve our next milestone. With my disease, I was believing things that were not working for me anymore. I needed a new belief. I had misunderstood something. I had misunderstood God. I had misunderstood preachers. I had misunderstood the results I was getting. I had misunderstood the illness. *Something* in my model of the world was incorrect, and I didn't know what. All I knew was that my belief system was not producing the results I desired. It was producing failure—or at least that was a piece of what was happening.

So I began to look at other belief systems, other theories for how things work in the universe. What do other people believe that is different from what I believe and that might be a better answer? I didn't know whether another belief would be a better answer or not, but I needed to look and see, because what I had was not working for me. So I had to look at questions such as these: Does God always want to heal people? Does God not heal people miraculously anymore? Did those healings ever happen? Is there better science about how to treat a disease that I don't know about? Is there an approved method of treating a disease or a treatment that works better? Is there an unapproved or unproven or experimental method that works better?

Existence has not been a 100 percent joyful experience. I have friends who are super happy and positive; they have no problems in their life, it seems. I mean, they probably have some trouble I don't know about, but from the outside looking in, everything looks pretty damn good. Finances are good, they've got wonderful families, nice houses, beautiful lives, and great health—no major pain in their bodies or drama in their lives. I don't begrudge them their good fortune, but I do think they've been lucky.

Part of me wants to say to these people, "You better look out, because you're overdue. Something's going to kick you in the ass." But of course, that's just my belief talking. I don't want to be that guy, either. I don't want to ruin other people's bliss by telling them to look out for the crap they're about to step in. Maybe it'll never happen. I just know that's not the answer for me, because I've had lots of pain and misfortune. I have an incurable disease that God hasn't healed. Positivity just doesn't cut it for me anymore.

So what do you do with this thing called reality? You become a scientist. You hypothesize that one belief will be better, then experiment. Just because you get a good result the first time, though, doesn't mean the hypothesis is true. You need to be able to replicate the result over and over again. And other people need to be able to do the same. That's the method. It's very rigorous. If I have a hypothesis and a theory, and I test the hypothesis with experiments, there must be repeated experiments that other people can duplicate and get that same result.

We can then all decide this is a good working theory. Next, we should share that theory with everybody, tell them that this is the best we've got so far, and then be open to somebody asking a better question. You decide: Is this the best hypothesis? Are these the best experiments? Are these the best results we can find so far? At this point, we can reach the place of having strong convictions, loosely held. I've done the work. I've experimented with many different hypotheses. And I found the one that seems to produce the best, most predictable, most reliable and repeatable results. And that's the theory I'm going to adopt for now. I'm always open to a better answer being just around the corner. That open-endedness is what bothers people, because everyone wants the ultimate answer right now—the 100 percent correct answer.

What do we do with beliefs? What else can you do? Beliefs are theories for how the world works, and when the world contradicts your theory, it's time for a new theory. You cannot believe whatever you want to believe. That is not how belief works. We all start with a sense of what we think is true. Call it intuition or your gut or divine insight. The point is that we don't really know how accurate we are until we start testing things. What we call beliefs are just habitual patterns of thinking. Before we can truly change our lives, we must examine our understanding of our beliefs, which can never be entirely accurate, only useful or not useful.

DO THIS

Make a list of beliefs you already know you need to examine or challenge. Usually, the beliefs we guard against examining are the ones we most need to put under scrutiny. No need to be dramatic about this; no one's going to force you to change those beliefs. But identifying the ones that might be causing you problems is the first step in limiting the problems. You might begin by making a list of all the beliefs you can think of and asking yourself a simple question: "Who told me this? How do I know this is true?"

Chapter 3

Beliefs Are Engines for Change

 The outer conditions of a person's life will always be found to reflect their inner beliefs.
—JAMES ALLEN

M Y WHOLE LIFE, I'VE ALWAYS wanted to be a writer. But when I first started thinking about writing as a way of making a living, I didn't believe I was good enough. Becoming a professional writer was such a lofty ideal, a nearly impossible dream. Then I discovered these people who wrote ads and made good money off them. *I could do that*, I thought. *I can write. I'm good enough at that.* At fourteen years old, I wrote my first ad for a radio station in Harrogate, Tennessee, called 7Q Country. The station was literally in the middle of a cow pasture and smelled like it. Once I got bit by the copywriting bug, I was a goner.

I grew up in the South, right at the buckle of the Bible Belt where persuasion was highly valued. Many people in my extended family were preachers, and every week they would stand on a stage, sweating profusely in the summer due to lack of air-conditioning, persuading us all of . . . something. That we needed to repent or we were going to hell. That the end was near. That Jesus loved us, for the Bible told us so. That we needed to pray more, fast more, read more, sing more, do more. It was all about using the right words to get us to do something.

I also loved television, spending hours a day watching shows such as *Bonanza*, *CHiPs*, *Star Trek*, and *Gilligan's Island*. I was especially fascinated by TV preachers, self-help gurus, and documentary shows such as *Cosmos* with Carl Sagan. It was all a persuasion game; not just the ads, but even the shows themselves were persuading us. *Star Trek*, for instance, clearly had a worldview to promote (a bright utopian future, where humankind had evolved and put problems such as money, warfare, greed, and so on behind us as a society). *The Andy Griffith Show* was selling a picture of the idyllic life of rural America (an idyll that many people would say was never real at all; ask people of color how they felt about those "good ol' days"). The point is: the commercials, the shows, the songs, the movies, the books—all of our communication is at some level either overt or covert persuasion. And while I was growing up, the people I knew who made a lot of money were by and large salespeople. Or they were entrepreneurs who were salespeople, such as real estate brokers. Everywhere I turned, I saw that success, influence, and the power to change things belonged to the persuaders.

So that's what I decided to do for a living.

One day after eleven years or so of writing copy for radio stations and others, I realized: I'm good at this. I'm good at persuading. I'm good at writing ads for radio. I was prepared from an early age to think about persuasion as a way of making a living. What carried me through my radio career, which spanned more than thirty years, was writing copy. Because I was the guy who wrote the ads for the Ford account, I was the guy you could not fire. The people at the local Ford dealership account would be pissed if you let that guy go. I was a radio disc jockey but wrote lots of copy for the on-air ad spots, and this endeared me to the salespeople who were at the fount of money in that business, and this endeared me to management. So I kept my job and did pretty well in that business. In the latter part of my career, these experiences gave me the backbone to stand toe-to-toe with top execs, calmly explaining to the marketing departments of Coca-Cola, Ford Motor Company, Home Depot, and other giants in the consumer business world how to improve the power of their marketing. I learned to persuade.

I became a copywriter and started teaching others.

What does a copywriter do? "The Carousel" scene from *Mad Men* is probably the best description. It's an iconic moment in American television that most people remember from the series, but whether you've seen it or not, I can think of no better illustration of this work that I've now done for many decades. The episode is called "The Wheel" because Don's ad agency has just landed Kodak as a client, and the company is shopping for the right fit to help it sell a new slide projector with that name. In typical Don Draper fashion, he takes the piece of tech home and plugs in a bunch of old photos from his life, trying to figure out what makes this thing so special. A common trope in the show is that the client never knows what they want; they need Don and company to show them. During the final scene, the world's most brilliant creative director advances each slide, narrating as he goes: "This device isn't a spaceship, it's a time machine. It goes backwards, and forwards . . . it takes us to a place where we ache to go again. It's not called the wheel, it's called the carousel. It lets us travel the way a child travels—around and around, and back home again, to a place where we know we are loved."

Kodak didn't ask for a rebrand; in fact, the company was quite explicit about wanting to keep the name. But Don Draper did what every great copywriter does: he changed the conversation, and the client loved it. Just as with his own life, Don deconstructed the whole thing and put it back together again at the eleventh hour. He created something better than reality, a truth worth believing. That's what a good marketer does.

I did the same with my life, learning very early on, as a teenager, that if I bought into certain things, they would help me go far. I understood the power of persuasion first as someone who was persuaded. When I was quite young, my mom took me to a real estate seminar hosted by Zig Ziglar. At the time, he was hawking the book *See You at the Top*. That was the first motivational speech event I ever attended, and I picked up a copy of that book, which was the first self-help book I ever read. Reading that book at the age of around fifteen, I was blown away, immediately realizing that thinking like this could get me far in life. So I started my own journey of self-indoctrination. I would buy a set of Zig Ziglar tapes, and then read the sales copy that went along with them. I knew I should read the copy because it made me believe in the tapes even more, which made me use them, which made me get the results.

Later, when I bought Tony Robbins's stuff, I remember printing out the sales letter. I didn't know that's what it was called at the time, but I read it ten times before I paid my first big amount of money to Tony Robbins. Years later, I would see other people do the same thing at events my team and I hosted. They bring the sales letter, printed out with notes in the margins. Now, I know what that is. That's a human being reinforcing their own worldview. They want to believe it's "worth it" because they want it to be true. I can relate. My journey is about me using the power of belief to create the life I wanted for myself, which was no longer borrowing other people's definitions of reality.

Someone asked Trappist monk and author Thomas Merton why he didn't become a Buddhist, because he became interested in mystical traditions at the end of his life, comparing notes with Tibetans about what he was experiencing. Here you had two completely different religious traditions—Catholicism and Buddhism—and Merton was seeing how similar they could be at the experiential level. Of course, Buddhists and Catholics have very different names for their experiences, but that's always the case with words, which are often what we use to communicate beliefs. When pressed about why he didn't convert, Merton said it was because he wanted someone to thank. And Buddhism didn't offer that, at least not in the way Merton desired. This is the reason we believe anything—because we want to.

Can you, however, believe in nothing? Can you choose to not be a believer? If our beliefs are not factual, then what good is believing in anything? If we are merely creating models based on the world around us, and they aren't actually correct, why should we believe at all? It's not that easy. In fact, it is impossible to not believe something. Try it. Remember that beliefs are thoughts you think are true, so can you choose to just stop believing something? I don't believe so. I mentioned that I had decided to believe a certain thing about my Parkinson's—that good could come of it—but the truth is I decided to consider it. It was a theory I wanted to test. I didn't have enough evidence to know whether it was true.

At the peak of my existential crisis, I started reading skeptics such as Richard Dawkins and Sam Harris. For a time, I gave in to nihilism, submitting to the meaninglessness of existence. If everything is an accident, I thought, then nothing is worth living for. Maybe it was true. I became despondent; there certainly seemed to be no reason for my disease. No matter how hard I tried, I couldn't seem to find a way. *Maybe I should check out,* I thought, secretly looking for methods to kill myself. It was a dark, hopeless time in my life, intensely unusual for anyone who knows me well. The idea I kept coming back to was Albert Camus's statement: "There is only one really serious philosophical problem, and that is suicide."

This was much more than an abstract question for me. After undergoing rotator cuff surgery on my right shoulder and suffering through a difficult recovery, I became dependent upon opioids. Such a surgery is one of the most painful a human being can have, and the most important postoperative recovery instruction is to keep the shoulder still at all times. You can understand how someone with Parkinson's disease might find that advice to be less than helpful. I endured several trips to the emergency room for surgery because of complications due to my tremors. For three months, I slept upright in a recliner, often in agonizing pain; I was unable to work—unable to do anything except sit in the chair and think about my life. One early morning, a little past two thirty, I looked down at the small table to my left and saw a bottle of Oxycontin, a bottle of Xanax tablets, and a glass of water. And almost instinctively, a thought appeared in my mind: *I could end all this pain right here and right now. There are lots worse ways to go.*

Obviously, I didn't go through with it, but at that moment, "checking out early" was more than a little attractive. Even at such levels of despair, though, I couldn't accept nihilism as ultimate truth. Despite my suffering, nothingness didn't make sense to me, even in the midst of reckoning with my mortality. After all, we are meaning-making machines. As humans, we tend to find patterns wherever we look, especially in our experiences, as well as in those who think and act like us. This is how we find a sense of belonging and significance. Personally, I found it difficult to believe that none of these patterns mattered; even when I was tempted to go there, I didn't like where that belief led. To put it bluntly, I was more interested in the story of my life having meaning than not—because the alternative made me unhappy. Whether the belief that nothing mattered was true or not was less important than whether that belief was useful. My nihilistic thoughts didn't make me happy, so I dropped them.

Why do I think believing in something is better than believing in nothing? Maybe you should believe in nothing if that's what gives you satisfaction. In my personal opinion, though, it's impossible to believe in nothing. We're going to believe in something, whether it's accurate or not, whether we admit it or not. So why don't we acknowledge that? We're going to believe in something, be it atheism, science, Taoism, nihilism, or that life is just a cosmic accident.

Are Your Beliefs Working?

How do you know if your beliefs aren't working? Over the years, as a result of earning my livelihood as a communications strategist and copywriter (not to mention my own intense self-reflection), I've noticed this question boils down to a handful of signs. If the following describes you, then it may be time for a change.

You experience repeated miseries. You repeatedly have the same feelings of loneliness, depression, or anxiety. You have the same relationship problems playing out over and over again or repeatedly experience the same money problems. These are all signs you have a belief that's not working; it's broken. For me, the belief that I should be healed, and that there was something wrong with me if I wasn't healed, produced so much misery that I ultimately had to acknowledge the brokenness of that belief. It just wasn't working.

You keep making the same mistakes. If you repeatedly make the same mistakes—drinking every weekday to the point of oblivion, cheating multiple times on your partner, watching too much TV at the expense of your health, making bad financial decisions, and so on—this is a problem. Everyone makes mistakes, but if you repeat behaviors that you see as bad or unhealthy, and you don't know why, chances are something you believe is causing you to engage in such behaviors. That's a sign that you have a belief that's working not for you, but against you.

You can't meet your goals. I'm not talking about just missing a goal once in a while; I'm talking about repeatedly missing the same goal over and over again. I set the same weight loss goal every year for ten years, and every year I failed. What was going on? I had certain beliefs that were not jiving with reality, which meant my feelings were not engaged, which meant I did not follow through on that goal. This pattern of setting and failing at the same goal over and over again is a strong indicator that your beliefs are out of alignment with reality.

You are depressed. As I mentioned, depression is the inability to imagine a positive future. It also casts a shadow of shame over the past and populates our memory with reasons to be filled with regret, bitterness, anger, and lack of forgiveness. It's very self-focused, disregards the feelings of others, and is often the result of too much introspection. I know I'll get arguments about that last statement, but it's true. At least I believe it is.

You are anxious. Anxiety is fear about the future. It's depression in reverse. It's thinking in terms of catastrophes, always looking at the worst-case scenario—visualizing it vividly and reliving it over and over again before it even happens, fearing what's coming next. Something you believe about reality is wonky. It's not working for you.

You are angry, bitter, or unforgiving. I'm not talking about temporary, momentary anger. We all have that. I'm not talking about a brief period of bitterness and forgiveness. We all experience that, too. I'm talking about wallowing in those things. If somebody did something to you twenty years ago and you're still angry about it, that's a long time to have an emotional reaction, don't you think? No matter how terribly that person acted, I would argue it's better for you to let go of that anger, that bitterness, that unforgiveness. You're holding the belief that keeping that anger, bitterness, and unforgiveness alive is going to somehow serve you. How is that working out for you?

You sabotage yourself. The final sign our beliefs are broken. This is a common theme I hear from a lot of people, and I certainly engaged in enough self-sabotage myself to know it's a real thing. Why do we continually sabotage ourselves? We say we want to do a certain thing, but we don't do the thing we want to do and end up doing the very thing we don't want to do. Why? The reason is that we have beliefs that are perhaps not broken, but in conflict with one another. If I believe that we all deserve to be prosperous and live wealthy, abundant lives, but I also believe that money is the root of all evil, I'm going to have a problem. I'm going to sabotage myself monetarily.

All of these signs are evidence of bad beliefs. Perhaps at some point, these beliefs worked quite well for you; but now, holding on to this old way of seeing the world is, in fact, killing you, robbing you of the life you could have.

Reckoning with Reality

A lot of unhappiness and angst comes from seeing the world inaccurately. We all have a sense of the way we think things should be, but life never perfectly lines up to those expectations, does it? Reality is not required to behave in accordance with how we think things should be. In my experience, what we call faith, in many ways, is simply a refusal to grow up.

Our beliefs stop working when the gap between what we expect and what actually happens gets so wide that the only sensible thing to do is to admit we were wrong. We all live in this space; some of us even choose to stay stuck in old patterns that no longer serve us because we were told living this way was good or admirable or holy. This, however, is a recipe for suffering. When we resist what our senses tell us because of what we "believe," we are clinging to a broken belief. And the result is suffering.

When I started writing down my beliefs, acknowledging that these were, in fact, the source of a great deal of pain for me, I saw that my blueprint no longer matched reality. And the contrast was stark. My diagnosis of Parkinson's brought such a clash between my own internal map for life and the actual territory of my experience that I couldn't reconcile the discrepancies. Many of the beliefs that had defined my core identity turned out to be unhelpful and, in some cases, even hurtful. I was beginning to understand what Sir Francis Bacon meant in *Novum Organum* when he wrote, "If a man will begin with certainties, he shall end in doubts, but if he will be content to begin with doubts, he shall end in certainties."

Beliefs either work or they don't. It's really simple math: When what you believe aligns with reality, the result is peace. When what you believe conflicts with reality, the result is stress, anxiety, even depression. But that's a bit of an oversimplification. A belief does not have to be perfectly true for it to be useful, and at the end of the day, what makes a belief powerful is not whether it's completely true or not, but what use it is to the person believing it.

But, of course, I didn't want to simply accept my plight of Parkinson's. I wanted, as we all do, to make sense of my suffering, to derive some meaning from my existence, no matter what. As Viktor Frankl wrote in *Man's Search for Meaning*, "Everything can be taken from a man but one thing: the last of the human freedoms—to choose one's attitude in any given set of circumstances, to choose one's own way." That's what was happening: everything I had clung to for so long had been stripped away. Now, I was left to find a new way.

What can a man do when faced with the decision to stop clinging to a worldview that no longer works? I had crossed a threshold from which I could not retreat, and I now had to decide which, if any, beliefs were worth saving—and which ones needed to go. More important, I had to figure out whether hidden in all this confusion might be a better way to live. The quest for better beliefs was on.

A Better Life Is Waiting

I'm not here to say that if you just have enough faith, if you think positively enough, you'll never have another problem in your life— quite the opposite, in fact. I held on to such a system for far too long, and it nearly destroyed my life. What I want to do is shine a light on the belief systems we unconsciously adopt that, in many ways, make our lives worse, not better, understanding how we got there so that we can rebuild a worldview that works.

Are your beliefs not working? Is there some pain in your life that is not helped by the way you view the world? Are you curious about what it takes to persuade anyone to do almost anything? This book is the story of the most painful, difficult experience of my life— and how it made me better. It's also the culmination of decades of my own research and practice as a copywriter and marketer; a skill

I never thought could save lives rescued mine. I didn't change my life by changing anything about my external circumstances. My life changed when my beliefs did.

And if that sounds easy, it's not.

Beliefs are engines for change in our lives—nothing more, nothing less. I don't know what made me sick, but I do know what made me better, and that was belief. I didn't get well in the way I expected or even in the way I wanted, but I did find a new way to live, and that changed everything. In the words of the inimitable John Mayer, "Everyone believes, from emptiness to everything . . . and no one's going quietly." As his song "Belief" suggests, letting go of bad beliefs is difficult and sometimes painful, but when we let go of the old, we make way for the new. It was belief that hurt me and belief that healed me, and how I changed those beliefs changed everything. When your beliefs aren't working, it's time to make your beliefs work for you. But we're getting ahead of ourselves. Let's start with ending what doesn't work.

Dumping Bad Beliefs

Most of us believe things because we've always just believed them. These beliefs feel safe, even if they aren't working—because the discomfort associated with change is often greater than the bumps in the road when life doesn't adhere to our expectations. This is called cognitive dissonance, and for most of us, it's a mild irritation, at worst. Sometimes, things just don't make sense, such as déjà vu or a glitch in the matrix; but often, our beliefs are useful guides. That is, of course, until so much crap hits the fan that we don't know which way is up anymore.

We all get triggered on occasion. It's in the wiring of our nervous system to see any threat to our worldview as a physical danger. Of course, this is ludicrous, but try to remember that at the next Thanksgiving dinner when you find yourself debating politics with an in-law who happens to live at the other end of the political spectrum. Or try getting into an argument with a well-meaning Christian about their views on the end-time. Inevitably, if we believe something that doesn't reflect reality, no matter how strongly we believe it and no matter how much we rearrange our life to make the belief seem true, we will nevertheless experience cognitive dissonance. This is a pretty good sign your beliefs aren't working. If what you believe is challenged by everyday realities to the extent that it causes you intense discomfort on a daily basis, then it may be time to change.

For me, the sense that everything was going to be handled with a swift miracle by Sunday made me unhappy. I held on to this belief so tightly for so long, and it made me miserable, even suicidal for a short while. My beliefs weren't working, not in any sense of the word. I needed a new paradigm, but I realized that getting one wasn't as simple as just believing another set of beliefs. We can't actually change our beliefs in an instant; it's a process of persuasion that takes time and evidence.

And lest you be deceived into thinking this is the perfect setup for a miraculous ending to this story, I still have Parkinson's. As far as I know, I still am going to die sooner than expected, be unable to control my muscles, and be more or less an invalid. But that's not the point of this story. The point is what happened after I learned my disease was not going away any time soon and how it affected not only my beliefs, but also what I believed about beliefs in the first place. Not only did my beliefs prove to be inaccurate; they were also unhelpful. Understanding this—and how to make my beliefs work for me—saved my life.

DO THIS

One of the best ways to examine our most deeply held beliefs, especially those that are damaging us in some way, is to ask, "What results has this belief produced in my life so far?" Be ready. This simple question can unlock a Pandora's box of epiphanies.

PART II

Amplify—It Gets Worse Before It Gets Better

If you've ever been numbed by a doctor or a dentist before surgery, you know that temporary alleviation of pain doesn't necessarily make it go away forever. Often, the next day, we wake up sore and aching, wondering what actually happened. This is where we are in the process of persuading ourselves right now. You want a better life? You want more freedom, joy, or love? It's time to increase the volume of your pain. You don't have to hurt more; you just have to feel the pain more deeply by imagining yourself at some point in the future deprived of what you ultimately want.

This is called amplification.

The next step in personal transformation is to amplify the consequences of not solving your problem, whatever it is. This step is the key to making a lasting change and is probably the most neglected part. What will motivate you to change your beliefs and behaviors? Realizing the cost of not attaining your desired outcome. In a word: *pain*. What is it costing you to not solve this problem? What will happen if you keep living as you always have? Allow yourself to go there, and on the other side of that discomfort, you'll find the change you seek.

Chapter 4

Turn Up the Volume

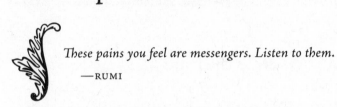

These pains you feel are messengers. Listen to them.
—RUMI

When I decided to let go of a belief system that wasn't working, the release was scary. I knew I was ready to let go, but I still needed to open my hands. That's where persuasion came in. As a copywriter, I had a framework for helping people change their minds. *Maybe,* I thought, *it could work on something as challenging as Parkinson's.* When it comes to trying to change a nearly impossible situation, we must focus on the problem and make it as unbearable as possible. There is no other way out but through.

What is something in your life that you cannot stand? The frustration this obstacle offers is the key to your liberation. Focusing first on the problem is an essential practice for any direct-response marketer. We have to get into the minds of our prospective customers and find out what is perturbing them, getting as specific as we can, using the exact words they'd employ to describe their pain. And if we are to persuade ourselves to a better life, we must do the same thing—use the most effective words and images we can think of to get us so sick of our situation that we're ready to change it.

This is simply a matter of asking the right questions. Copywriting is all about pinpointing the pain someone feels and offering a solution to fix it. Naturally, when my life was nearly unbearable, I employed this same method, beginning with two simple questions.

Question 1· Where Is the Pain?

This is the first and most important question to ask and a sticking point for a lot of people. There are plenty of peer-reviewed studies that demonstrate we're more likely to make a big change in life to get out of pain than we are to move toward a state of pleasure. This is Freudian Psychology 101, but until recently we've misunderstood how exactly our brains are wired.

As Nir Eyal, bestselling author of *Indistractable: How to Control Your Attention and Choose Your Life*, has said, it's not a mixture of pain and pleasure that motivates us, but purely pain. From a neuroscience perspective, our brains evolved to avoid discomfort. It's how we stay alive. That's why even in the least dangerous situations, we can still feel fear that threatens to paralyze us. Even pleasure, as perceived by the brain, is really just avoidance of pain, whether that's boredom or physical suffering. So knowing exactly where it hurts, how it hurts, why it hurts, and how it's going to get worse is important. It's really important to get clear about our pain; otherwise, we just have a vague sense of discomfort but don't know why. That's the reason people don't change. They know they don't feel good, but they don't feel bad enough to figure out why they don't feel good.

Thinking about pain—giving it structure, form, definition, and words—makes it feel worse, so people don't want to think about their pain. But that's the very thing we have to do to get rid of the discomfort. You have to clarify what it is you're dealing with. The Emotional Freedom Technique (EFT), or "tapping," teaches something similar. Perhaps you're familiar with EFT; in this practice, you acknowledge the beliefs or thoughts that are causing you pain or discomfort by saying them out loud while tapping on certain acupressure points. You repeat things over and over again until the emotional charge of those statements is gone, and they become just words. You get over something by going directly through it and not avoiding it. Some people swear by this approach, and I'm not sure if it's all a placebo or legitimate science. Personally, I've wondered whether relief comes not so much from the physical tapping but from directly confronting the horrible things you think about yourself when you say those words out loud.

We do the same thing in copywriting and marketing. Of course, we have to approach this in a way that customers will accept as palatable. We can't just barge in the room and say, "Your life sucks. Here's why you suck. You should buy our stuff. It will fix how much you suck." That's not an approach that's likely to work for most people.

Question 2· How Deep Does the Pain Go?

In Ayn Rand's classic *Atlas Shrugged*, one character says there's a point where the hurting stops; it only goes so deep. In my life, that's been true. The hurt goes only so deep, as unimaginable as it may seem. There is always an end, a point at which the pain is not touching the core of who I am. As the conscious observer of my life, I can see the pain, feel it, even experience it, without being fully affected by it. There is some part of me—call it a soul or a consciousness or just a deeper form of awareness—that is able to perceive such stimuli without *being* them. Yes, I still get upset even when I'm in this Zen-like state. But the pain doesn't go as deep as it used to cut. I know, even in the midst of my worst moment, that it's not going to last. This discomfort, however slight or unbearable it might be, is not going to seem important to me a year from now. A temporary cash flow problem or restriction of travel won't seem like a big deal in a few years. Everything is relative, even pain.

There are other forms of suffering, however, that do linger. We think about them years after the fact, and they still cause pain. These deeper pains are good to recognize, because hidden in them is some of our greatest potential transformation. People sometimes get upset with the copy I write, saying I'm always focused on the negative. "What's wrong?" they wonder. "What's the problem? Does there always have to be a problem?"

The answer is, of course, yes, there does. In life, there is always a new problem; so, in a business, if we want to sell something, we have to appeal to this very evident reality of life. Otherwise, people won't believe you and therefore won't buy anything. People say they just want something better. But that's not enough. If we want something and still don't have it, there's some deeper pain we're not dealing with. And if we want to create true and lasting change in our lives (or in the lives of others), we've got to face our pain and know just how far down it goes.

Don't Reward It, Record It

How do you know something hurts? You get honest. You can journal or have a conversation with a friend. I keep a private daily journal that I don't share with anyone. Usually, I record an audio file, then transcribe it into a digital journal entry, and eventually delete the entries because I don't want anybody to read them. These entries are my musings on where I am in life and what hurts right now. When I address where the pain is, that's the first step toward creating a better life. In my journal, I write my most honest thoughts, regardless of how embarrassing they are. This is an important part of acknowledging reality, including what's happening inside you. The only way we're ever going to be able to solve our problem is by first naming it.

Something I do most mornings is to write down everything that I'm thinking about for that day or week or what's coming. I'll do my best to be as honest as possible with myself about what I'm thinking, even if it's not necessarily pleasant. Then when I've written everything down, I'll stop and look at what I've written. I'll ask myself, "Which of these thoughts do I really want to cultivate? Which of them do I want to change?"

Changing beliefs comes down to changing what we think about, because we tend to believe what we think over and over again. In his bestselling book on psychology and persuasion *Influence: Science and Practice*, Robert Cialdini wrote, "Often we don't realize that our attitude toward something has been influenced by the number of times we have been exposed to it in the past." A belief is simply a repetition of an idea that we think is true; when we hear something over and over again, we start to believe it. Writing down our problems, however, is not necessarily a repetition of a belief. It's acknowledging the voices already swirling around in our minds and trying to identify where they came from, then choosing to rewire them.

By writing down our problems, we use this acknowledgment to create positive change. We aren't dwelling or focusing; we're confessing: *This is what hurts, right now, and I don't like it.* So what does the world look like once the way you perceive this problem is changed? I can't eliminate Parkinson's disease, but I can shift the way I think about it. What's good about that? What does that make possible? It's not pain itself that motivates us as much as it is our perception of pain. Our perceptions shape our experience of reality, so whether your pain is legitimate or not, if it feels painful to you, it is.

When it comes to how we perceive and process pain, there are grooves in our brains that are worn pretty deep. We may think we deserve to suffer or that such pain is normal or even good. But we cannot ignore the discomfort, the gnawing suspicion that life could be better. When we dwell on the thought that this is the way it should be, we stay stuck. What I advocate for is being more conscious of what you're thinking and making a decision about whether it's good for you or not.

What to Do with Pain

I realized my Parkinson's wasn't going to go away. In fact, I had to face the fact that it was going to get worse. And I had to ask myself, "What is that going to look like?" Was there anything I could do? The ultimate end of the road with Parkinson's is pretty clear for everybody: near total disability, the inability to help oneself, to feed oneself. People don't die of this disease, but they die with it. And they usually die for corollary reasons, the most common being pneumonia, when food gets sucked into the lungs because of choking while eating. Officially, the person died of pneumonia, but the person really died because they could no longer swallow or breathe properly as a result of Parkinson's.

Another common outcome is dementia. I had to face the fact that my most prized possession, the thing I was most proud of and felt was most valuable about me—my intellect—was possibly going to be taken away from me eventually by Parkinson's. Of course, my intellect is definitely going to leave me someday, because one day I'm going to die, and my intellect will not exist on the physical plane at that point. But the chances that I will develop dementia are about 50–50. I happen to have the gene that's an indicator of being much more likely to develop Alzheimer's or dementia. I looked at all those possible terrible outcomes, and then I asked myself, "Is there anything I can do to mitigate, delay, or alter any of those outcomes?" And that's what led me to make a lot of changes in my diet, exercise routine, and even things I focused on. I knew there were things that I could do that would not cure disease but that could postpone the time when I'm completely disabled and ultimately die.

The problem I was trying to solve didn't shift, but I abandoned my original solution, in which the only "salvation" was just to be miraculously healed. In that way, my situation did shift. It was the same problem: physical disease leading to physical and mental decline, loss of quality of life, and ultimate loss of life. The solution I envisioned was delaying or reducing the progress of the disease to preserve and improve the quality of my life for a longer period of time, for however much time I have left. But really, if I'm being honest, my problem wasn't Parkinson's; it was my thinking, *I can't seem to get rid of this thing*. When I finally accepted reality, I was able to change it. I became optimistic. The question changed from "How do I fix this?" to "How can I learn to live well with this?"

I discovered it was possible to delay or even halt the progress of the disease in ways that are backed up by science and proven by the experiences of others. In doing so, I bought myself more time on

Earth. Perhaps in the intervening years I bought myself, researchers will come up with a cure, a genetic treatment that reverses the effects of the disease and stops it in its tracks. Or maybe I will simply get to enjoy more of life while I have it.

It Takes Pain to Change

It never ceases to amaze me how much we can suffer before we are really willing to change. What I've learned is the only way to really change is to allow the pain to get acute enough that we have to do something about it. This doesn't have to be a passive process, however; we can find ways to consciously amplify our pain so we don't have to hurt too long before we change.

In the months after my diagnosis, somewhere between denial and faith, my wife and I loaded up our motorhome and left for a road trip to Glacier National Park. Let me tell you, if you want to go somewhere to be depressed, Glacier National Park in October is a great place. It's cold; the leaves have fallen; and it's rainy, snowy, empty, and miserable. We went there with our two pugs, and the only time we went outside was to take them to relieve themselves in the gray, muddy cold. The whole time, I stayed inside the RV reading books on healing, wondering, *Why am I not experiencing these things I'm reading about in these books? Why am I not seeing the healing I've heard about at big church services and rallies? Why am I not able to use my positive thinking to get myself out of this hole?*

One day during this trip, Lynn sat me down in our RV and said, "I need to talk to you." We were knee to knee when she put her hand on my arm and said, "We need you to pull your head out of your ass." What a thing to say to a sick person! I have a degenerative disease and every reason in the world to be depressed! She continued, "You've got to stop indulging in this victim mentality. You've got to stop wallowing in depression. We need you to step up and be the leader you were before this happened. We need you to lead your family. We need you to lead your business. We need you to lead your customers and your audience. These people are counting on you to be who you really are, so you've got to pull out of this. Whatever you have to do, you've got to find your way out of it, and you've got to do it now. It can't wait."

I'd like to say that from that moment on, I was different, that I was able to instantly change my thoughts and feelings. But I wasn't, and I didn't. It was, however, the day when things began to change for me, the turning point when I started realizing what I'd been believing was not helping me. All these books and prayers were not doing me any good. I felt inadequate to the problem I faced, and all this material was only making me feel worse. The implied message, as far as I could tell, was this: "If you're still having the problem, you're the problem." The stakes were getting higher. I was getting sicker, and I was falling into a deep depression.

I had a decision to make. I could sit in the unbearable pain of the belief, or I could find out what was really motivating me and try to find something better to believe. Previously, my belief in positive thinking and healing prayers had helped me level up in life, but now this belief was preventing me from getting what I wanted, which was peace and happiness. I needed to believe something new. Nietzsche said, "He who has a *why* to live can bear almost any *how*." I believed that—mostly—and wanted to figure out what my *why* was now that my world had been turned upside down.

But was I willing to do the work and make the hard changes?

More Pain Means More Change

I lied to you a little (but I'm in advertising, so you probably saw that coming). Pain, in itself, doesn't create change. In fact, we are used to living with so much pain and discomfort that we think it's normal. We deserve this, we think. It is what it is. Whether that sense of resignation comes from a Western Judeo-Christian perspective—the biblical "thorns and thistles" argument for why life can be so hard—or from an Eastern karmic explanation, we all know how to suffer. But suffering sucks. If something hurts and you're not doing anything about it, that's because it's either something you can endure or you're just not paying enough attention. Turning up the volume on what hurts expedites our ability to change our circumstance.

Amplification for me meant realizing I was going to die and leave my family with nothing. If I only saw my disease as a burden and my future as a disaster, I would waste my life, business, and talents. Perhaps amplification for you means understanding that if you never lose weight, you'll have a heart attack and die at fifty. Maybe it means you'll never be able to play with your kids or go on hikes or live a long and happy life. Get specific about what your situation is really costing you, and you'll get to a solution even faster.

How do you amplify your pain?

You ask yourself one crucial question: "What will life be like if I don't solve the problem?" Since getting Parkinson's, I've become a bit of an amateur neuroscience geek, and one of the things I've observed is that all the latest neurological research shows we are only ever motivated by pain. Even pursuit of pleasure is really just an avoidance of pain. So let's use the pain to our advantage. Amplification is about imagining what happens if you never solve this problem, if you never get out of your own way. What does life look like twenty years from now? For me, it meant realizing I was going to die and leave my family with nothing. The fear of squandering my remaining days eking out a mediocre existence on Earth was enough pain to motivate myself to think and act differently. The immediacy of those feelings forced me to change.

Amplification works because we are masters at denying reality. We tell ourselves it would be better if we saved money for our future or took better care of our health. But that's not enough to change your behavior, because what's more real to you is the cappuccino you're drinking and the sugar in it that makes it delicious, or the cheesecake you're eating, or the television show you're watching instead of exercising. That's more real to you than what will happen five or ten years from now.

Most of us, as soon as we're aware of a problem, don't immediately solve it. We put off solving the problem, because that feels good—at least in the short term. We smoke cigarettes, even though we know they cause lung cancer, because the jolt of nicotine feels good. It gives us some energy or quells the discomfort of not smoking. People may say, "I know cigarettes cause lung cancer, but I enjoy smoking! My grandpa smoked till the day he died, and he lived to be one hundred years old." But that's just a lack of imagination. You don't think about what it's going to be like when your lungs are hunks of rotting meat that no longer supply you with enough oxygen. You don't envision how excruciatingly painful and horrifying that's going to be. You don't imagine that it will be so terrible you'll actually think, *I want to take my own life rather than continue to endure this.* Turning up the volume on the pain is how you avoid worse realities in the future. You have to take it to a point where you don't just tell yourself, "Maybe I should stop smoking cigarettes." Rather, you say, "Oh my God, this is killing me." And with that awareness, you change.

Earl Nightingale said, "We become what we think about most of the time, and that's the strangest secret." When we think about our pain over and over, it often becomes more pronounced. Pain is a signal from the body to the brain telling you something's wrong. If you're hurt, your body will essentially communicate, "Help! We need to stop this. We need to change something—now!" Granted, some pain is more bearable than other pain. Whether it's a mild back discomfort or a headache or maybe even a cavity, human beings have the perseverance to withstand many discomforts. This is adaptive; it allows us to survive, because we can't always drop everything to address our pain. Sometimes, we have to keep going. But this same ability to persevere can keep us from getting what we truly want.

When we learn to live with lack, whether that be a lack of health or wealth or some other desired goal, this is not optimal. It's not pain in itself that causes us to change, then; it's how we perceive the pain. I was grappling with Parkinson's, trying to make it go away. When it didn't go away, I had to change how I felt about it. I wasn't just trying to see the good and be artificially optimistic. I asked myself: "Do I have to wake up every day feeling like crap about my circumstances in life? Can that be the problem that I'm solving?" The fact is, I frequently do wake up feeling like crap, and then I have a choice to make: Do I want to keep feeling that way? No, I don't. That hurts. Acknowledgment of the pain allows me to reconsider what it means to me. Amplification forces me to change it now or at least the meaning I give it.

DO THIS

This may scare you a little, but I encourage you to write a vigorous, imaginative worst-case scenario describing how deep the pain is going to go if you don't change something. Pick a singular issue to work on and really go all out in "amplifying" the pain you're going to feel if this continues unchanged. If you do this exercise with maximum intensity, I predict you'll automatically begin feeling change. It won't all be automatic, however. But this should get you started down the road of transforming whatever it is that needs improvement in your life.

Chapter 5

People Change When They Have To, Not When They Want To

 We do not have a fear of the unknown. What we fear is giving up the known.

—ANTHONY DE MELLO

IT WAS LATE AT NIGHT. My wife was asleep, our dogs snoring softly in the bed beside us, and I was awakened by a rumbling of "voices." *Who do you think you are, trying to run a business when you're so sick? How can you pray for the healing of others when you're not healed yourself? If people really knew who you were and everything that's wrong with you, they'd never listen to a word you had to say. You might as well kill yourself.* I bolted upright in bed and looked around. My heart was pounding, and I could barely catch my breath. It felt as if another person were in the room with me, talking to me, whispering in my ear. I roused myself out of bed and went to the kitchen to get a drink of water. Terrified, I began to pray.

At this point, I was right in the middle of those early days of struggling with Parkinson's, in that liminal space between believing that every disease was a form of demonic oppression and the possibility that this belief might not be working anymore. I found my way to the living room and sat on the sofa for a while, reading the Psalms, trying to get my bearings. Have you ever noticed that the veil between the natural and supernatural worlds seems thinner in the wee hours of the morning? I don't believe this is just my imagination. Maybe it's something about the middle of the night or circadian rhythms or something else, but we seem to be more open during this time of half-wakefulness. At any rate, I felt particularly sensitive that night. My heart was tender and open; I was scared but also felt anchored in my faith. As I read and prayed, my nerves calmed, and peace enveloped me. I went back to sleep and woke the next day feeling rested.

I didn't know what, exactly, had happened; but it felt like an attack, something personal and malevolent. This was not the first time I had experienced such an attack, and it wasn't the last. Over the years of being a Christian, an agnostic, and a skeptic, I have wavered between thinking of what evangelicals call spiritual warfare as a literal battle, filled with scary spirits; special incantations to chase the devil away; and, well, utter nonsense. I've also experimented with every explanation in between—including psychological trauma, sleep terrors, or maybe just my own inner demons. But at that time, I was pretty sure a demon was attacking me, and the belief that I could pray away the attack—something I had been trained in and practiced for many years—worked. I believed a thing, and that belief allowed me to go back to sleep.

As we have seen, our beliefs are always changing and evolving, serving us until they don't. And then, we have to consider the possibility of letting them go, trying something new, or maybe even returning to what we always believed—but with new levels of awareness. As our beliefs evolve, we have to be open to new ways of seeing the world. I have always been a pretty impressionable person; I love exploring new ideas and seeing how they fit my current model for reality. I also love exploring new ways of seeing the world, but I feel especially drawn to science. I have to see the evidence for whatever it is I want to believe. This has often felt like a fault, a weakness of mine. Couldn't I just accept things without needing to see the evidence? What was wrong with me? Why was I such a doubter? Over the years, I've realized this isn't necessarily a bad thing. All belief begins with *openness*; you cannot believe something new without being willing to see something you previously missed. To let in new information, you may have to let go of some old belief you were once certain was true. What we need to live our best lives, as far as I can tell, is an openness to both admitting when we might be wrong and accepting something we've never heard before. This is the endless experiment of belief.

Brainwashing Yourself to a Better Life

For most of my adult life, I have been a big fan of personal development gurus such as Tony Robbins and Jack Canfield. Ever since my teenage years, I have studied the work of these two men and others, reading their books, attending their seminars, and even getting to write copy for some of them. These coaches hosted events that opened me and others up to something new and transformational, and many still swear by the efficacy of their methods. Most attendees entered these events enthusiastic about becoming an entirely different person, and they often left feeling that they got what they had hoped for. Whether or not the changes they experienced lasted is not for me to say, but the experiences themselves were curious.

As I dug deeper into this world of personal transformation, I began to see that a lot of the tools and tactics these teachers used at these events had certain characteristics in common. For example, the seminars often consisted of incredibly long days—twelve to fifteen hours, in a single room with limited breaks—for three to five days in a row. During this time, people would become more psychologically pliable: willing to change some of their deepest beliefs and longest-held thought patterns, able to set incredible goals and somehow accomplish them. It was incredible to witness, almost magical, and I wondered whether the patterns I noticed were coincidental or intentional.

Another one of the techniques involved in almost all of these seminars is that at the event (usually in the middle or toward the end of the second day), the personal development trainers will sell you an upgrade to the experience: a membership to a "platinum" mastermind group, access to some secret "inner circle," or simply a ticket to the next event. Because you are so worn down and excited about the experiences you've had thus far, you are more willing to say yes to some new experience. Your beliefs are malleable now. You are more persuadable, and they know that they can get you to do almost anything at this point, even change religions or leave your romantic partner.

For those who "invest" in whatever next step is available, a common tactic after this is that the teachers will have you make a list of all the people you know who would appreciate this experience, then ask you to call and tell them about it: "You should come do this, just as I have. It's the greatest thing ever. It changed my life." The trainers want you to make those calls while you're there at the event, while you are in the heat of the process. It works better that way. You have now become a convert to their cause, and as you proselytize to others, your convictions only deepen. You wouldn't tell the world about something you didn't absolutely believe was true, would you?

This is the way religions and self-help movements get born, and after I had seen several of these events, they all started to look the same to me. These methods, however, are nothing new—especially in the personal transformation industry. Almost every method and tactic you see used in this space has the same origin: *est*, which stands for Erhard Seminars Training, named after the founder, Werner Erhard. In the early 1970s, est was the original self-help seminar, the transformational experience everyone was raving about that eventually attracted celebrities, movie stars, and even intellectuals. It was the place you went to for a long weekend and came back from with a different persona, raving about the experience to your friends.

One person who was drawn to these wildly popular and somewhat controversial seminars was Dr. Sheridan Fenwick, a graduate of Cornell University and professor of psychology at Columbia University. Having heard so much about these experiences, she was both skeptical and curious about the methods being applied. Because everything she had heard was from secondhand sources, she decided to go directly to the source and see what the fuss was about. Her goal was to attend one of the seminars, objectively study the methods, and then document the process and report on it. Her experience, however, was part academic and part personal. In spite of her desire to remain an objective observer of the process, Dr. Fenwick couldn't help but get a little carried away by what she experienced in 1971. Over the course of a few days, she was surprised to see how she was pulled into the experience, even though her intention was to infiltrate the process and understand the methods, if not expose them. It wasn't that easy, though.

The first thing Dr. Fenwick noticed was that the trainer intentionally treated attendees who were grown adults as if they were children, telling them that there were certain rules during the seminar and not explaining why. This tactic, she says, is sound psychology when one is persuading people to change the way they live their lives, as she wrote in her book *Getting It: The Psychology of est*: "If you don't give people reasons, they have to invent their own and in the process of doing so will choose the explanation that to them is most convincing."

This is the most effective kind of brainwashing—you don't even know it's happening and would swear to the opposite. In this case, the facilitator doesn't have to make you do anything; you do it to yourself. If you're joining everyone else at a Tony Robbins event jumping around screaming, it must be because you want to, not because someone forced you. You chose this behavior that you would never otherwise do but somehow found yourself performing in a new and unfamiliar setting, because, well, everyone else was doing it. Still, it was your choice. That's not manipulation—*is* it?

The next thing she saw was that no one was being forced to endure these long days if they didn't want to. In fact, the facilitators continually offered attendees the option to leave the seminar at any time and get a full refund. This, too, Fenwick says, is not what it seems: "If people have voluntarily committed themselves to an action, they will increase their liking for that action and will be more likely to internalize the attitudes, standards, or values that their action has implied." The fact that attendees at the event were offered multiple opportunities to leave might seem noble but was another way to keep the attendees bought into the process: "Your sense of having made a voluntary commitment to be there is bolstered. You could have left but you didn't, and if you didn't, then you must want to be there. Once you have convinced yourself that you are there because you want to be, your receptivity to the content of the message is at a high point."

Other tactics included restricted access to bathroom privileges, limits on the amount of sleep attendees were able to get (due to the long days and early mornings), and harsh confrontations between the facilitators and attendees. The days were incredibly long, ranging from fifteen to twenty hours of instruction and application every single day. Some nights, attendees would go to bed around three o'clock in the morning, only to be back in the same room the next morning by eight for the next session. The sleep deprivation, authoritarian environment, and restrictions around basic human needs such as food, sleep, and bathroom visits started to wear on people. But instead of getting angry, people grew more anxious and, in many cases, began to experience what appeared to be dramatic experiences they would later call breakthroughs and tell all their friends about. Staying somewhere difficult and continually choosing not to leave leads human beings to rationalize all kinds of things. This is how we make meaning out of our most painful and uncomfortable experiences, the especially difficult ones that we cannot change. We have the sense that it all must matter, that it couldn't have been for naught. So we ourselves provide the meaning.

Dr. Fenwick, of course, wasn't the only skeptic. Many people attended these events unsure of what to expect but curious about the hearsay, only to return completely transformed. These methods were the forerunner to personal transformation methodologies that would soon become commonplace in the modern self-help movement, utilized by everyone from self-help gurus to television preachers. But even Werner Erhard, the godfather of the modern self-help movement, was not the originator of these methods. They go way back, beyond the 1970s, to sources you could even call *ancient*.

As I saw this sort of thing unfold at personal development seminars myself, I realized the formula was something familiar to me; I'd seen it my whole life. The music, the long, drawn-out services that required you to sing and shout and move around, the speaker sometimes offending or challenging you and making you uncomfortable, the invitation to stay, the request to go deeper: they are all part of one of the oldest forms of persuasion the world has ever seen. And the formula reminded me of what people in the southern United States used to call "revivals." These arduous experiences require people to opt in by attending a service that is often outside or in a large arena. The whole thing is free, so you are obviously there voluntarily, and you are invited to raise your hand, move your body, or sing along. All these are small ways of getting you to open up, to choose to engage in a deeper process, often culminating in an invitation or "altar call," in which you are encouraged to make a commitment. In the old days, preachers would often have audience members come forward for prayer or healing and sometimes even fill out a "commitment card" reflecting whatever decision they'd made—choosing to follow Christ or get baptized or recommit their lives to God.

I saw the same thing play out in megachurches, as well, especially in the "signs and wonder" movement, in which miracles and healings are almost promised as outcomes of the experience. In both religious and personal development settings, the same kinds of tactics kept popping up. Preachers and speakers alike would conduct long services and seminars—six, seven, eight, nine, ten hours long— where they would play trancelike music; employ fog machines and lights; and sometimes even use darkness and guided meditations, prayers, and prophetic "words" for people.

By the end of a three-day experience, you would often feel you had been transported to another world and would be very moldable. Then, you might be encouraged to go evangelizing and recruit others to the movement. Sometimes, you'd even be encouraged to leave the facility and tell others the good news you'd just received. In other words, you'd go find "fresh blood"—more souls to save, more lives to transform. And the process would just repeat itself, because the speakers created a self-feeding mechanism in which their very customers were self-made salespeople. It's a brilliant way to grow any movement, and if it all sounds familiar, it should. This is also the way pyramid schemes and multilevel marketing companies are structured.

Lest I sound jaded, I believe most people involved in most of these movements had and have good motives, that their zeal is authentic. This was true for est, as well. Dr. Fenwick, after her four-day experience at the seminar, had in some ways become a convert to the cause. "I took the training," she wrote in her book. "It was an extraordinary experience. And I have some serious concerns about the implications of the est phenomenon. I think people ought to know about it. I think people ought to *think* about it." People, of course, did more than think about it. After the publication of Fenwick's book in 1976, another hundred thousand people—many of whom were both public figures and mental health professionals—attended the seminars. The est phenomenon also created an abundance of critics, some who dared to call the seminar a form of mind control, even going so far as to label the organization a cult. Due to a number of controversies, including someone dying at one of these events, est eventually had to close its doors in the mid-1980s, rebranding itself and moving on to gentler forms of transformation that didn't involve practically locking people into hotel conference rooms for twelve-hour days, psychologically abusing them, and letting them believe it was all their own idea.

Once I understood the psychology behind these experiences, many of which I'd subjected myself to in both religious and non-religious settings, I felt a bit gross, ashamed that I had been so easily manipulated and, worst of all, that I had done it to myself. But, as Dr. Fenwick says, "est doesn't need to 'brainwash' people. We all do it to ourselves every day." She's right. The trick is to become aware of what we are doing to ourselves, what we are allowing ourselves to believe and the life we are living as a result of that belief. Much good came out of my experiences with what some may call mind control. I've been brainwashed, if you want to call it that, more than once in my life, and often for the better. But when the greatest crisis of my life hit, I realized it was my turn. I was now the one holding the keys to the bathroom doors, if you will. I was the one making the rules. Now, it was my job to become the brainwasher, and Lord knows I had the training.

Almost all of the so-called experts and gurus in the self-help world today are employing the tactics that Werner Erhard first codified so many years ago. I learned them from as many sources as you can count and saw the same methods employed in the development of my own faith journey. What I learned from all these people, whether they were teachers or preachers, was the same lesson, over and over again: if you want to change your life, you first have to open yourself to the possibility of change, then introduce a new way of looking at the world. If brainwashing yourself sounds scary, that's because it is. The best way to get brainwashed is to be willing for the brainwashing to happen, acknowledge what you're getting into, and be the one who does it. A lot of people have lost themselves in such pursuits, so let's make sure we do this right.

Why You Should Change

At some level, people have to want to hear why they should change. If someone isn't seeking transformation, you're not going to have any effect on the person with anything you say. It's possible that by telling the person a good story, you might open up their subconscious mind to the idea of change: *Maybe I'm wrong about this. Maybe I should think about this more.* That's all it takes—a little openness—for someone to be willing to think about it. Then, you ask the person, "If you're thinking about changing this aspect of your life, why would you do that? What would be a good reason for doing that?"

When I'm coaching someone, I ask them: "If you were 100 percent decided that you wanted to change . . ."

Then they might say, "But I'm not 100 percent decided."

So I say, "Okay, pretend that you are 100 percent decided. That you know absolutely, 100 percent, that you want to change. Why would that be? What would convince you of that?"

"Well, if I was totally convinced that if I kept eating this way I would have a heart attack, then I would want to change."

"Let's talk about that. What will happen if you don't change your behavior?"

"If that theory of eating is right, I'll develop atherosclerosis. My arteries will harden, possibly crack, maybe burst. Maybe I'll have brain damage. Maybe I'll have a stroke."

Then I continue to walk the person through the consequences, asking questions like these: "Empirically, what would that be like? Where will you be when that happens? What will it feel like? What will happen to your family? What will happen to your finances? What will happen to the things you wanted to do with your life?"

Once you admit that something needs to change, and you ask yourself why you need to decide, the reason has to be strong enough. That means you have to realize the consequences of not changing. What's the cost of complacency? What's the cost of denial? For most of us, the cost of denial is the issue. It's easy to deny that eating a piece of cheesecake will kill me—because the cheesecake is so good. *How could it be bad? It hasn't hurt me so far. I ate the whole cheesecake last night. I'm not dead, right?* Not yet. So we continue to believe the old story—which is really just a series of beliefs unfolding through a narrative structure.

We say we want to change, but we don't. We don't like the way we handle our money, or the way we eat, or the way we exercise (or don't). The problem is that changing seems more painful, at least in the moment, than not changing. But the truth is the opposite. It's going to be more painful in the long run if we stay the same. The bad things that are going to happen are going to feel a lot worse than the good stuff feels right now. You don't want to get fired. You don't want to shave twenty years off your life. But all those probabilities are not tangible to us in the present. So we stay stuck.

This is how we make sense of our lives: *I've done it this way for so long, so it can't be wrong, right?* That's called a "narrative bias," which means that just because someone has been doing things this way, it's the way things should be done. If I got cancer, then started eating an apple a day, going for a walk, and getting chemo, I might turn around and say, "If you do these things in exactly this order, you'll survive cancer, too." But that's crazy. Maybe what actually led to my hypothetical healing had nothing to do with that sequence of events. It doesn't matter, though. Humans love the simplicity of a story: *If you do this, then that happens.*

Storytelling is a powerful tool, because we understand ourselves as characters in the story of our lives. So when we hear a good narrative, we see ourselves right in the middle of it. There's nothing wrong with this tendency—it's how we're wired—so long as we see the inherent flaws in such a bias and find ways to use it to our advantage.

It Takes a Breaking Point

Whether they take the form of a self-help seminar, a charismatic revival, or a political rally, events designed to motivate people all rely on techniques used in large-group awareness trainings (LGATs). The term "large-group awareness training" comes from the Human Potential Movement, which was a marriage between the counterculture movement of the 1960s and the human desire to succeed. LGATs use tools such as jargon, self-hypnosis, relaxation techniques, and neurolinguistic programming during marathon sessions to help attendees remove major roadblocks in their journey toward their best selves. Don't get me wrong; this stuff works—I've used these techniques myself. And the outcome is often positive; this is how we train soldiers and get people to stop eating themselves to death, after all. But these techniques are also the way cults are formed.

The point is you have to get someone to a breaking point before they're even willing to change. It is not enough to be open; you have to be broken into receiving new information. This is the reason, I think, that mystics go off by themselves in the desert or spend days in a dark cave meditating by themselves. Scholar Carmen Paglia talked about these experiences in her lecture "Cults and Cosmic Consciousness: Religious Vision in the American 1960s": "Marathon, eight-hour sessions, in which participants were confined and harassed, supposedly led to the breakdown of conventional ego, after which they were in effect born again." Born again! She's not talking, mind you, about a Southern Baptist big-tent revival service in rural Mississippi where you are compelled to come forward at the end of a multiday set of services to confess your sins and receive healing, forgiveness, or whatever the preacher is selling. She's talking about a personal development seminar, but she could just as easily be talking about a military boot camp or a college fraternity pledge week.

The method is the same in all of these settings: to get an individual to change, get them around a bunch of other people who will, in some ways, make it more uncomfortable to stay the same than to simply change. That's not all, though; you've got to get the person out of the comfort of their own environment, introduce them to a new "tribe" to which to belong, and spend numerous consecutive hours breaking down the individual and rebuilding them around a new belief system. To put it bluntly, whatever the brand, whatever the form of change being offered, you have to brainwash the person.

All belief is brainwashing—and the good news is we can use this technique on ourselves.

Imagine Your Worst Nightmare

Pain is subjective. What's painful for you might be exciting to me. Before we can change anything, we first have to acknowledge our pain and really feel it all the way through. We have to face the reality of our situation and look at what happens if we don't change. We have to make the pain worse, which really means "de-numbing" ourselves from what is already happening.

The only way to truly change your pain is to sit in it—not to deny it, and not to pretend that it's not real or that it's somehow less bad than someone else's suffering. You have to just acknowledge how much it hurts and feel the pain all the way through, as deep as it goes. All our forms of wishful thinking and positivity don't allow us to feel the pain; they bypass it. Avoiding your pain is denying your reality, and you always know when you're doing so. Your mind may believe its own story for a while, but your body knows differently. This is the reason that positive thinking, as we typically understand it, doesn't work. It ignores the loudspeaker in your life that won't stop until you address it—that is, pain.

Be mindful of the pain. Realize this hurts like hell, or it's really going to hurt if you don't change something soon. This process begins with actually feeling your pain. We are all motivated to avoid things that hurt, so we can use this wiring to our advantage. As I said before, as a part of this experience, you come to realize the pain only goes so deep. It's bad, but it's not as bad as you thought it might be. Fear exists to keep you alive; and if you aren't dead or bleeding out on the floor right now, then there's still time to make a change in your life.

How do you make the consequences of a situation real enough now that you are actually motivated to avoid them? You have to visualize vividly, with as much feeling as possible, a future that involves your not having solved your problem. You have to imagine your worst nightmare and bring it into the present as if it's already happening. People often say, "Don't worry about the future!" That's all well and good, unless you are in a situation you don't want to be in or are stuck in a belief system that is slowly killing your soul. Whether it's a financial goal, a health aspiration, or the desire to spend more time with our kids, we all have things about our lives we wish were different. The best way I've found to start taking strides in a more positive direction is to get really negative. In other words, you've got to worry.

There's value in revisiting this exercise often. I do it once every quarter. I go back and look at my goals and the things I'm working on, which are derived from the desire to make things better. I look at my reasons, and those always start this way: *Well, if I don't actually make this amount of money, save this amount of money, reach these health goals, then here's what will happen.* And I write out what will happen this year, then in five years, then ten years from now. That's always a pretty bleak picture, which stirs up enough emotions in me to want to make some significant changes now.

Your current situation may feel bleak, but we can harness it into motivation to change. We move away from pain; that's how we're built. The process is not binary, but a continuum. Ideally, we are moving through life with less and less pain. This is what we call success or pleasure, but really, to our brains, it's all about pain reduction. And we often have to feel the utter intensity of our pain, amplifying what hurts and imagining how bad things could really be, before we can finally experience the transformation we want.

Using It Without Abusing It

The challenge we face, then, is discerning behavior that could be manipulative from behavior that can help us create an environment that facilitates a breakthrough. Maybe there's no difference except our awareness of what's happening. Certainly, there's nothing wrong with using music, lights, and speech patterns to create transformation, whether it happens in a church, at a self-help seminar, or in the comfort of your own home. The difference is whether or not you are conscious of what's happening. This, I think, is the difference between Billy Graham and Charles Manson. There's nothing wrong with inviting people into a brainwashing experience that'll make their life better, so long as they understand what's going on.

All society, in some manner, is based on this concept: to belong, we have to give up some of our own individuality. Even the very concept of the social contract, on which most democratic governments are now based, is this principle in action: give up part of yourself to get something greater. That said, we have to know what we're getting into. Granted, everyone makes mistakes, and many people misuse truth for selfish purposes. The evidence of past abuse, of course, is not necessarily a sign that a particular technique itself is wrong or immoral. All I'm saying is we have to carefully examine the motives of the people to whom we are trusting our lives. We have to take control of our own transformation; otherwise, we may be tossed back and forth from one brand of brainwashing to another. I know, because that was what happened to me.

After years of chasing healing circles and attending self-help seminars, I realized this approach wasn't working for me. In the throes of my greatest health need ever, all the positive thinking and praying didn't seem to be doing much good. And I realized I'd been brainwashed; I'd given up my own agency and intuition, because it was easier to let someone else tell me what the truth was than to go through the painful process of figuring it out myself. But I started to wonder: maybe all those years of attending seminars had some value. When I experienced my own existential crisis after being diagnosed with Parkinson's, I became curious. Could these teachings I'd studied for decades, and had admittedly become quite skeptical of, help me in some way? If I had believed all kinds of crazy things because of the sound of a song or the words of a minister, could I use these same tactics to change my current situation? Could I brainwash myself into a better belief system? I didn't know for sure, but I was open to the possibility. And that openness is all it takes.

DO THIS

My client Tony Robbins says it well: "People don't get their *shoulds*, they only get their *musts*." We all have things we know we should do—behaviors we should change—but often this change only happens when it becomes an absolute must. I suggest taking one behavior, belief, or habit you want to change and writing out at least ten reasons why you must change. Try writing it out in this form: "Change _____. Or else _____." And see how much more motivated you feel.

PART III

Story—Believing in a Better Future

The method for changing your life is a familiar one. It is something we have all been exposed to since we were little children. Every time you watched a cereal commercial or read a magazine or talked to a car salesperson, you saw this process in action. If we want to live a better life, we have to first acknowledge the beliefs fueling the negative forces we are experiencing. And we must learn to let go of those bad beliefs and adopt the skills we need to begin believing better things. Now, the rubber meets the road. We've laid the groundwork, and the next step is the hard work: we must persuade ourselves to believe something better. This is persuasion.

My whole life and career, I had been preparing to persuade myself to change my beliefs, without even realizing it. To believe anything, you must become open to new possibilities, walk yourself through the scientific method that allows you to play with new beliefs and new ideas for how you think reality works, and then choose the beliefs that work best for you. I've used this method to sell seminars, books, radio ad spots, and everything in between. In getting people to do something, the method works pretty well. So why not use this same sales process to sell you and me on the best possible life we can imagine? It just might be as easy as a shepherd leading his sheep home.

Chapter 6

The Power of Myth

 There have been great societies that did not use the wheel, but there have been no societies that did not tell stories.
—URSULA K. LE GUIN

YEARS AGO, I SAT IN an enraptured audience at a seminar filled with eager, hopeful, weepy-eyed marketers like myself. Okay, nobody was weeping, but they were coming close. There was a palpable energy in the room, a buzzing feeling of possibility. We had all registered for this conference wanting something, and each speaker gave us what we paid for: hope. This particular speaker gave us an exercise, however, that caused me to rethink everything I thought I knew.

"I want you to write your life's story, plot point by plot point . . ." he said.

Great! I thought. *I got this.* I had already begun scribbling in my notebook: *Ray Edwards! A humble man with humble beginnings rises up through minimum talent, adequate adversity, and ample wits to become THE GREATEST COPYWRITER THE WORLD HAS EVER SEEN!*

"... And I want you to make it a tragedy," he finished.

I put my pen down. Although a tragedy wasn't the story I wanted to write, I was able to write one quite easily: *Man is born. Man becomes a great copywriter. Man gets Parkinson's. Entire life falls apart. THE END.*

This exercise is crap, I thought. *My life already is a tragedy. I don't need to write a story about it. It is what it is.* Then, the speaker turned the tables on us.

"Now do the same thing," he continued. "Write out your life's story, but make it a heroic triumph."

A triumph. A triumph is what I had begun writing the first time, but that was surface-level stuff. What the speaker was asking me to do was challenging and uncomfortable; heck if I knew what the triumph over Parkinson's would be. Wouldn't triumph be just beating the disease? And then something clicked. My life's story is just a story. It's not my life. It's not fact or reality. It's just a story. And if I could tell the same story that I had previously understood as a tragedy and make it a triumph, then maybe things weren't so hopeless.

The stories we tell ourselves are the ones we believe, and we repeat what we think is true. But the fact is our lives could change in an instant if we were able to shift our perspective on the circumstances surrounding us. I turned the page and began writing my story again—everything I had experienced up to that very moment. This time, it was a triumph, for real. It was still the same story, still the same major details, but I remembered little things I had forgotten, tiny blessings and gifts, as well as hope about how all this could turn out. Maybe, for the first time, my story would be something I could rely upon—something useful.

When considering the story of your life, you can write it as either a tragedy or a triumph, depending on how you choose to see it. Which story, then, is actually true? The one you believe; the one you fully embrace with your whole heart and cling to. Sometimes, we need to see our current situation as a plot point in a much deeper story and take it all the way to the end to see how it's going to play out. Think about the action or behavior you know you need to change but are reluctant to. If you can project this same activity, continued ad infinitum into the future, then you can use your imagination to consider what your life might be like ten or twenty years from now. It might not look so good. That's great. That's the motivation you might need to finally make some major changes. Seeing the facts of my story and where it was leading if I didn't change a few things woke me up. This is the gift of telling a good and convincing story— to yourself and to others. The story can change everything.

Good Stories Have High Stakes

Just this morning, I did not feel like getting up and going to work. I almost fell coming up the steps to get to the office. I almost spilled my coffee all over the inside of the car because I was shaking so badly. During a Zoom meeting, I was sitting on my hand the whole time to keep it from shaking. I don't want to show up when I'm like this. But there are consequences for not showing up, and properly understanding the stakes of any story is what makes it interesting.

When we think our story is a tiny blip on the radar of history, we tend to believe our actions don't matter. But when we see our life as a high drama, packed with action and important choices, we make decisions more carefully. And the truth is there is a consequence for every choice we make; some of these consequences can be quite devastating. I'm not saying that you should worry about every little thing you do, but if there's a major change you want to make in your life and something is standing in the way, it may be time to reimagine your situation as a dramatic narrative and consider the costs of not succeeding.

I used to appear in public only when I could control the shaking. But at this point, it happens so often and so intensely that I can't count on being able to control it. I have to get more comfortable with showing up just the way I am. And that sets a whole set of consequences in motion. I think, *If I show up this way, what are people going to think? Are they going to think that I'm just getting sicker?* Well, yes, of course they are. Because that's exactly what's happening.

I have to ask myself, "What are the consequences of not showing up anymore?" Decreased income; decreased impact and influence; and having to live with the consequences of feeling that if I can't show up and be who I really am, then I am trying to perpetuate a lie. If you looked back at my past videos or listened to my past podcasts, you'd think, *Wow, you're doing great!* Well, that's because that video you just watched is from a year ago.

I went through this same exact thought process this morning—thinking about what would happen if I didn't show up. I could have made excuses. But ultimately, part of the journey I am on is getting more comfortable with just showing up. This process is very real to me, because I go through it almost every day. Though it may feel better in the moment just to bow out and say, "Nope, can't make it," it won't feel better in the long run. Self-care means holding yourself accountable. You know when you need to hold yourself accountable.

The day I decided to go public with the fact that I had been diagnosed with Parkinson's took place long after I received the actual diagnosis. Up until that time, I had told myself that it would be better if I kept the diagnosis to myself, because people who knew the diagnosis would write me off as if I were finished. So then I started telling myself a different story. What if I didn't go public? What would be the cost of keeping my Parkinson's a secret? The cost would be that I would begin showing up less and less ably, and nobody would know why. Some people at the time had already been asking me whether I had been drinking. If I continued to keep the diagnosis a secret, I was just going to appear to be getting more and more erratic, unreliable, undependable, and incompetent. And none of that was true. The cost of not telling my story was that people were going to make up their own story.

And then on the other side, if I did tell, the same things might happen. They'd say, "You're unreliable, undependable, less competent." But perhaps I could show them differently. Maybe my openness about my diagnosis would also inspire other people not to give up if they had some similar situation in their own life. Maybe I'd be able to inspire someone to rise above their circumstances and achieve something more than they thought possible. So that's the story I told myself, and I went public. I had both results I'd imagined, in fact, with some people saying, "You're done," and others being quite encouraging. But by that point, these reactions didn't matter. I had already asked myself, "What's the worst that could happen?" And the worst was everyone would make those assumptions, and some people did just that. And what would that mean? That would mean the pressure would be off. I wouldn't have to do anything. Then, I could believe, and maybe do, anything.

A Tale of Two Men

Robin Williams passed away by suicide; the man who brought so much joy and laughter to the world couldn't find enough of those treasures for himself. His death devastated me. I won't follow the footsteps of the many who have called this action selfish or who have in some other way judged him for taking his own life. His death seems a tragic loss, but I am unable to pass judgment on how much suffering another man can tolerate.

I did love Robin Williams, though. When I was a boy, watching him on *Mork & Mindy*, I was inspired by his comic genius. He would go on to touch my life through many films. Like many others, I identified with Robin Williams and his view of the world (at least as I perceived it). I felt connected to him, even though we had never met, so when I heard the news of his death, it was a blow to my soul. The impact, however, took on even greater dimensions when I learned that he had Parkinson's disease.

In the wake of Williams's death, his widow revealed he'd been recently diagnosed. Many believed this was the final blow that caused him to despair. The news of his diagnosis was especially significant to me, because of my own. Like Williams, I chose to keep my condition secret for as long as possible. I was shocked to hear about him, because he was the second actor with whom I felt a close connection to be diagnosed with the disease. The other was Michael J. Fox.

I was a Michael J. Fox fan back when he was on the sitcom *Family Ties*, and of course through all the *Back to the Future* films, the sitcom *Spin City*, and most of his other work. I probably saw every film he was in. In the charming, bumbling-but-admirable characters he often played, I saw myself. I felt that we grew up together. When Fox publicly announced his diagnosis and left the *Spin City* cast, I remember thinking, *That poor bastard. I feel so sorry for him.* Then I forgot about him. For a while.

When I was diagnosed, my initial symptoms were mild, and my diagnosis was swift and surreal. I went from being the "normal guy" who had no health problems to being "that poor bastard" with a daily pile of pills that kept my body functioning in a seminormal fashion. I immediately recalled how horrified I had been when I learned of Fox's condition. Now I was living out the same story. That's when I began to notice my old "pal" Michael J. Fox again. He has been an icon to many in the decades since his initial diagnosis, demonstrating what it means to keep living, keep loving, and keep contributing, even in the face of a daunting challenge.

And this leads me to my point. What I saw when I first came across these two stories was two potential paths for my life. I could check out—and honestly, I've thought about it a few times—or find a way to keep going. It took the starkness of these two stories and my own understanding of what my choice might mean to my loved ones for me to decide what kind of story I wanted to live.

What Story Do You Want to Live?

In all of my workshops, I take a page from that story-writing exercise and ask the audience members to write out the story of their life twice. The first time, there are only two rules: the story has to be true, and it has to be tragic. Then I have them write the story a second time. This time, the rules are that it has to be true and that it has to be a happy hero's journey. Finally, I ask the participants, "Which story is true?" They always answer the same way: they are both true. The story of your life is not your life; it's just a story. And stories rely greatly on who's telling them.

Stories are subjective. History is written and rewritten by whoever ends up winning. The story belongs to the hero, not the villain—and who gets to decide which is which? Well, whoever's telling the story. When we think about the story of our own lives, we are completely in charge of the meaning we make out of it. We can't control what happens to us, but we can control what we do with those experiences. What we believe about our life is a matter of how we choose to see it. And there's almost always another perspective.

Using stories to persuade people is a necessary and essential skill of any copywriter. I've worked with my own clients on understanding this principle—that you can use almost any story to make any point you'd like. But I have to use this process in my own life, as well. Just the other day I had an episode of dystonia, which is an effect of Parkinson's that causes all the muscles in your leg to tighten up so you can hardly move. It's like having a charley horse from your hip to your toes that gets so bad it feels as though your bones might break. I sat on the floor of my hotel room for thirty minutes before I could function again.

At that moment, it was very difficult to think, *This is an adversity that will help me become a better person.* I wanted to just give in to the other thoughts: *This sucks. I'll never get relief. I hate this.* But I didn't give in. I knew the dystonia would go away, because it always does. While I do not wish this disease on anyone, I would not be the person I am without it, and for that I'm grateful. There is always a better story to tell. You can't always control the circumstances, but you can shift the story you tell about it.

What Makes a Story Great

Stories are about what people want to believe. We watch and read stories that promise to reinforce our beliefs and give us hope. People look for things that reinforce their version of reality. We cling to stories because our brain is wired to acquire accurate information about our surroundings. When we have decided that we know what's accurate, we begin looking for more evidence to support that view of reality and for ways we can use that view to get what we want. Once we decide a story we tell ourselves is true, we're going to hold on to it strongly. It gives us strength. It's an important and well-evidenced belief.

Great copy is not just about making good rhetorical arguments. As persuaders, we have to think about the beliefs people have to buy into to realize that buying our product is the right thing to do for them. This is how I start most copywriting projects, especially for big-ticket items. There are certain beliefs people must buy into before, for example, giving you ten grand to coach them. First, your prospect must believe the coaching is worthwhile. That's a belief you have to reinforce or create. If a coach is good at what they do, the audience needs to see evidence. But that's not enough. The audience members have to see themselves benefiting from the coaching themselves.

If what you're selling requires difficulty (as in the case of a CrossFit membership, for example), you have to get the audience to believe that the results are worth it. You do so by telling stories of people just like the audience members who've done what they're seeking to do. You then demonstrate that this—and only this— product is the answer to their problem. By learning how to use this methodology on yourself to change your own behavior, you can empower yourself to decide what life you want to lead.

Two Foundational Elements

Every change we need to make in life must be reinforced by two foundational elements. First is the logic of the argument. Why do you want to change? How will your life get better? This is typically the sort of thing we consider persuasion, but this is only half the equation. Second are the stories that make the belief not just theoretical but bring it to life. I don't need to just believe that doing exercises and taking supplements will lead to optimal health; I need to hear stories of people who have achieved that result performing those very actions.

There are different stories that resonate deeply with us, so by discovering what story lines resonate for us, we can incorporate these elements into our own story. We can consume stories about people who have overcome obstacles and become victorious, if that's what we want to do. If we want to achieve a different goal, we can look for stories that support that viewpoint. The stories we tell ourselves are what we believe, and we tell ourselves the stories we *want* to believe. So choose which stories you take in carefully. They just might become the life you end up living.

Shifting the Story

This brings us to the *S* in PASTOR: "story"—that is, the story we choose to tell ourselves about our life and how we can consider the events in our life as ways we've overcome problems to achieve success or as barriers to getting what we want. *S* also stands for "solution." Once you have described the problem and amplified the consequences of not solving it, it's time to find the solution to the problem. This comes down to choosing to believe another perspective is possible. In other words, you have to believe a new story. Equally important as imagining your worst nightmare come true is considering the opposite. Now that you've considered the consequences of your current actions, let's take a look at the alternative.

What happens if you do solve this problem? What pain gets relieved? What discomfort is alleviated? How is your life made better? What does it feel like to move away from this thing that is causing you to suffer?

For me, what I visualize is being a relatively healthy eighty-year-old person. Maybe I still have some problems. Maybe I'm not super mobile, but I'm not completely disabled. And I'm very sharp mentally. When I meditate, I visualize both my ideal future and what happens if I don't change. I use amplification to turn up the pain on the beliefs and behaviors that are preventing me from getting to where I want to be; then, I tell myself a story about what life will be like when I am relieved of that pain and experience the success I long to have. If you want to change something, you have to visualize the outcome you want with as much clarity as you envisioned the pain. You make the outcome real enough that you desire to step into this better future, which will make all the pain and discomfort go away. Solving your problem comes down to understanding this process and choosing to believe another story is possible.

What would your life look like if you could change it completely? How would life be different if your problem were solved? What does the solution look like? What you're searching for here is not just an answer, but hope that things could be drastically different. Remember: The story of your life is not your life. It's just a story. What we tend to believe about the story we call our life is really just a matter of how we choose to see it.

DO THIS

You probably don't realize this, but time travel is a reality and you've been doing it all your life. You can only go forward, though, and that's the catch. To really make a difference in the quality of your life, often what is needed is to "leap forward" on the timeline. Write a story about your future life the way you want to see it. Write it out in detail. Don't worry about how you're going to make it; just describe in great detail what your life is like in the future. Where do you live and with whom? What do you do for a living? The more detailed you can make this story, the better. I suggest writing in present tense as if you're already living there. Describe your house, your car, your job (if you have one). The more vividly you can imagine this future, the clearer it will be and therefore the easier it will be to grasp.

Chapter 7

When Old Stories No Longer Serve Us

 That's how stories happen—with a turning point, an unexpected twist. There's only one kind of happiness, but misfortune comes in all shapes and sizes.

—HARUKI MURAKAMI

A MAN CAME TO A THERAPIST, convinced that he was already dead. The therapist looked for increasingly creative ways to help him see that he was, in fact, not a corpse. She asked him whether corpses bled, and he said no, so she then stuck his finger with a needle. He looked at his bleeding finger and said, "Oh my God! I'll be damned, corpses *do* bleed!" We are all at least a little like that man: capable of holding on to the most ridiculous beliefs even in the face of overwhelming evidence to the contrary.

This is easier to recognize in others than it is to see in ourselves. If you confront people who are deluded in their beliefs, they'll typically become even more entrenched in what they think is true. Even if what we believe is ridiculous, we become defensive whenever confronted. That's just our posture as humans. If someone challenges us, we immediately feel threatened and will instinctively want to defend ourselves and our position. When we hear a story about a man who thinks he's a corpse, however, we think, *How ridiculous—that guy is deluded.* We are blind to our biases—until life finds a way to break through.

One way to shine a light on the truth is through the power of narrative. This is why Jesus taught in parables. The religious people of his day wanted him to teach what was "empirical," using the Torah as their common rubric, but he refused to do this. Instead, he wanted listeners to think about flowers and birds and farmers. He told stories, because a story can have many meanings without having to be explicit about any of them. What is the meaning, after all, of *Star Wars* or *Gone with the Wind* or *Romeo and Juliet?* We can ascribe any number of meanings to these tales, all of which may be different and in their own way true. Which one is the right interpretation of the story? The one we believe. Storytelling bypasses our so-called rational defenses against new information (which, incidentally, end up manifesting in some pretty irrational behaviors, such as ignoring other people or even hurting those who challenge our beliefs). A story helps us become open to new ideas.

We, as a species, are averse to novelty. Homeostasis is our modus operandi, so we tend to fear outside-the-box thinking. This is why Jesus said, "He who has an ear, let him hear." *If you understand what I'm saying, listen. If you don't, then never mind.* It's worth noting he usually said something like this following an aphorism, some philosophical or theological insight he was sharing. When he told stories, he let them land however they would with the audience. Stories can change us, but only if we're ready to change.

According to Dr. Joe Dispenza, about 60 to 70 percent of our thoughts are based on our stories—who we've been in the same, familiar past. We become chemically addicted to a certain emotional state, because that's how we've felt our whole lives. But he teaches that personality, which we often think of as ourselves, is really just a learned behavior. It's a habit, based on old data that may or may not be true, practiced over and over again. Sometimes, those neural grooves go so deep that they become addictions, entrenching us into old ways of being that don't serve our well-being anymore. After all, what is an addict but someone who did something for a while that felt good until it started to severely harm them? To recover from such an addiction takes effort, discipline, and sometimes loving support from a community. In some cases, addicts feel as if letting go of a certain behavior would kill them: "I need this." Sometimes, they're right. Sometimes, an addict can't quit cold turkey, or their entire body will rebel against them. What they need, then, is a gradual weaning from their addictive behavior so they can believe another way of being is possible.

So it is with us and our own stories. Dispenza's premise, backed by lots of credible science, is that thoughts trigger the release of certain hormones and neurotransmitters, which create an emotion. You have a certain cocktail of these chemicals that cause you to feel a certain way: happy, angry, depressed, horny—whatever it is you're feeling. We tend to become habituated to a certain emotional state. This is not a new idea; people have been expressing it for decades, since the dawn of the positive-thinking movement. Our habitual emotional state is a chronic thought pattern—but it's also a chemical addiction. You count on that feeling to feel certain that you know who and where you are. It's scary not to know who and where you are.

If you want to experience something different in your life, identify the current cocktail you're addicted to. Recognize that what's causing it is that you keep thinking mostly the same thoughts every day. Dr. Dispenza runs through an example: You wake up in the morning, and the first thing you do is roll over and check your phone, scrolling through Twitter and your newsfeed. All those familiar actions help you reconstruct the person you think you're supposed to be today. You get all your familiar problems, worries, and stresses going. You get a rush of cortisol. It's the place you go to habitually. Angry people tend to be angry all the time about everything. Happy people tend to be happy all the time about everything. Suspicious people tend to be fearful and suspicious. In most cases, it's not because they're naturally wired that way, but because they have wired themselves that way.

In some cases, people have neurological problems with their brain that cause certain things to happen. They didn't think themselves into this condition, and they probably can't think themselves out of it. But these cases are rare—maybe 1 to 2 percent of the population. It felt a lot better when I was not part of that 1 to 2 percent of the population, but that percentage remains fairly accurate, as far as I can tell. It's impossible to change an addiction without replacing it or forming a new positive habit. That sentiment is at least as old as Jesus, who said that if you cast one demon out and you haven't swept the place clean and filled it with something else, then seven more will come in and take that demon's place. That was pretty good psychology for a guy with no technology.

The danger is that some people are going to decide that what I mean is that we should just make up anything we want to believe that makes us feel good and then go with that. But that's not my approach. I'm not suggesting people believe any fanciful thing that makes them feel better, because that can also be a road to disaster. I believe we should try to be as accurate as possible in our beliefs. We've got to be willing to continuously sift and sort through the information given to us by our five senses and decide: *Is this still* true? Does it work on a factual level? Is it helpful and useful to me? If it's not true and useful, then how do I need to adjust my belief to make it more so? We have to assume we're never 100 percent accurate, because we're most likely not. This is very unsatisfying for people who want to be absolutely right. I'm one of them. I love to be right, and I love for people to know that I'm right. But life is not about being right or wrong. It's about making the most of our time here, finding meaningful ways to contribute our skills and time for the benefit of others and ourselves.

Reframing Reality

So how do we shed our old stories so that we can live a new one? Hale Dwoskin originated the Sedona Method, which is an emotional release technique. If you have something you are holding on to, imagine that you could take that belief—that you're somehow defective or chronically anxious or whatever—and just drop it. Imagine you're holding on to a pen, and then you simply drop it. Most people's first reaction would be this: "Can it really be that simple?"

And Hale would respond, "What if it were? Could you possibly let go of it?"

"Yes, I could possibly let go of it."

"Would you let go of it?"

"Yes, I would."

"When?"

"When" is the invitation. It amazes me. Every time I tell someone about this exercise, they laugh because they realize the answer could be "now" if they wanted it to be. That's the whole teaching. My wife, Lynn, and I went to Hale's workshop in Sedona. It made a huge impact on both of us. To this day, we'll ask each other, "Are you holding on to that belief?" Usually I'll catch her before she can even ask me the full question, and I'll say, "Yeah, yeah, I got it." We even joke about it and abbreviate it, saying quickly, "Could you, would you, when?" We've used this technique thousands of times. When we're caught up in something, we'll ask each other if we could let go of it. Sometimes the response is "I guess I could." And then the other will ask, "Well, if you could, would you?" Then we realize what the other person is doing.

Beliefs are reinforced by the stories we tell ourselves, even if humans are unreliable witnesses. We can create almost any reality we want, if we want to badly enough. Granted, we may not be able to wish away cancer or Parkinson's or even a bad marriage. But we can reframe what this thing means in the story we are living. And this reframing begins with a willingness to see things differently.

It's a challenge for us to reframe and reshape the stories that have guided us through life. And so when we consider persuading ourselves to live a better life—whether that means losing weight, making more money, or dealing with an incurable illness—what we're really doing is getting ourselves to admit the possibility of a different reality. And doing so is hard, because we become addicted to familiar stories, even if they aren't true or even helpful.

As happened for many people, in 2020 a plethora of poop hit the fan for me. We suffered a huge financial setback because a lot of our customers canceled their contracts. I realized there were some weaknesses in my business structure. I had shoulder surgery, which went as expected, but it was much more difficult to recover from than I had anticipated. During this time, I could do nothing. The recovery was much more painful and difficult than I had imagined, especially since I wasn't supposed to move my shoulder, and keeping it immobile was impossible due to my condition. I was put on opioids, which caused me all sorts of problems and were tough for me to get off. So when I talk about addiction, I'm not speaking metaphorically or clinically. I've been there, felt my body craving a thing I knew wasn't good for me in the long term. I also had two emergency room visits and a blood infection. The experience was hard in a lot of ways.

Yet it was my best year ever in terms of spiritual development. I faced what my current beliefs were and how they were working for me. Writing this book helped me understand so much about myself, including how I navigate through life and how certain beliefs I'm still clinging to may no longer be serving me. This is a continual process. It's not about ever figuring it all out; it's about playing with models that work for a while and then stop working. It's about looking at the lenses through which you view life—what we call "beliefs"—and finding ways to reframe them when they're no longer working for you.

During that year, I experienced a lot more connection and growth in my marriage, especially during the weeks and months after my surgery. I was stuck at home and unable to move around much, so I saw no one except my wife. We spent many evenings at home, with the fireplace roaring, and we talked and read to each other, sometimes for four, five, or six hours straight.

It was beautiful. We talked about marriage. We talked about having children. We talked about religion. We talked about our beliefs. We talked about the things we did and did not agree on. We talked about the nature of love over decades. We talked about everything—all the stuff we had been afraid to talk about, the good and bad, including one question in particular in which I had a great deal of interest: "What happens if one of us becomes permanently disabled?" This idea scared me, and the honest conversation about it brought so much healing. What we keep in the dark haunts us so much more than what we bring into the light.

We talked about death, decline, and decay, and at first it was very difficult. I wanted to do all the things I normally did on a daily basis—such as driving to the coffee shop and getting an espresso, going for a hike, or completing a workout—but I had to face up to the fact that many of those things were distractions from my true presence.

When you slow down and replay the details of your story, you may find yourself seeing things you missed before. You may realize a relationship you thought was ending simply entered a new season, or perhaps it had already ended a long time ago. If you pay close enough attention, listening to your life as theologian Frederick Buechner encourages us to do, you may discover all kinds of mysteries worth beholding. And you may see things that no longer serve you, that need a reframing of some sort.

For my part, these conversations helped me see how driven I was by external success, how I would put scores up on the board for other people to applaud, and how doing so didn't always make me any happier or even more successful. During this time of healing and honest conversation, I grew deeply, in many ways that were impossible for others to see. My ability to deal with unexpected things outside my control improved. In business, we discovered that growth through constraint was possible by focusing on one thing at a time and doing it in the simplest and most efficient ways.

Which One Is True?

When I was probably eighteen or nineteen, I was pretentiously into absurdist books with cult followings, as one is at eighteen or nineteen. One quote from the book *Principia Discordia*, written by Greg Hill with Kerry Wendell Thornley and others, really stuck out to me: "All statements are true in some sense, false in some sense, meaningless in some sense, true and false in some sense, true and meaningless in some sense, false and meaningless in some sense, and true and false and meaningless in some sense." I would say that statement itself is also true or meaningless in some sense. Truth and meaning depend on the value you attach to a statement.

This perspective is the heart of my experience with Parkinson's disease. Any time we experience a tragedy, there is the event itself, and then there are our memories and the stories we tell ourselves about the event. They are a confabulation that hide or accentuate the tragedy. I'm not saying we make things up on purpose; but there is a difference between the stories we tell ourselves and the actual thing that is happening. Sometimes I make a big deal out of something really small. And other times I brush off something that was probably a bigger deal than I made it.

Reality can be whatever you want. How do we know? Just take a look at the proven fallibility of memory. Human memory is quite unreliable. We are all really unreliable storytellers of our own lives. There's a lot of research on the unreliability of eyewitness testimony and the controversy over repressed memories. People can ask you questions about something; our brains abhor a vacuum, so they fill in the part that is not remembered. I like to ask my wife how she remembers something so that we can see the difference between our memories. We like to joke about me being an unreliable witness. This frightens a lot of people, of course, because they wonder, "Well, then who can we trust?" To which I say, "Nobody—least of all, yourself." Then the question becomes "What do I do with that? If I have a memory about my life, this thing that happened, or this ax that I'm grinding, what do I do about it?" That's the place where we can get down to asking, "Is this helping me or hurting me? Is it useful to me or not useful to me?" If it's hurting me, it's hurting my relationships, my financial security, or my health. Maybe I should investigate the possibility of eliminating this thought pattern. But if it's not hurting me, who cares whether it's true? People don't believe stories because they're true; people believe stories because they're powerful.

Persuasion, quite simply, is selling possibility. And one of the best ways to introduce new possibilities to a person is to tell a new story. But sometimes, we first have to let go of an old one. For me, I was telling myself that I was a loser and was going to die, disappointing everyone I loved. Of course, all of these facts were, in a way, true. I *was* going to die, probably sooner than I realized. And I was overweight; in debt; and, well, kind of a loser. But that was just one way of telling the story, and after years of living this way, I saw that it wasn't working for me anymore. It wasn't helping. I had to try to find a new frame.

Consider how you're telling your own story right now. Is your life a tragedy or a triumph? Is that story serving you? Is it empowering your mental, physical, emotional, and spiritual health? If the answer is no, then why would you want to hang on to such a story? Wouldn't you prefer to have a better one? And then, the objection becomes "But what if that's not the true story?" So let's get clear on something: the story you're currently telling yourself is also not true. Neither is true. They're just interpretations of what happened. Stories we tell about our lives are beliefs. And as we've already established, a belief is simply a model for reality. It's an approximation of the truth. When a belief is no longer grounded in reality at all, we have to let it go, adopting something that is hopefully truer and more helpful. So which untrue story would you rather hold on to—the one that helps you or the one that hurts you? Every story is true in some sense, false in some sense, and meaningless in some other sense.

Stories are not about truth as much as they are about finding a frame for reality that is helpful to the audience. This, by the way, is also a good example of how titles, adjectives, and facts alone tell us underwhelming details about a person. They can't give us the essence of who someone really is. How you choose to tell the story, in many ways, *is* the story.

DO THIS

Here's an opportunity to transform some painful event from your past into something different. This is not fantasy. This is not denial. This exercise has delivered real healing for me and can do the same for you. Pick one unpleasant incident from your past, preferably something about which you have a story you have told many times. This may be one of your favorite stories to tell people as you get to know them, about some tragic event that makes you the way you are now. Pick the thing you think is the "worst thing that ever happened to me," and then suspend your disbelief and write a little essay called "How This Was Actually the Best Thing That Ever Happened to Me." Make it all true. You might be surprised at what you discover.

PART IV

Testimony—Evidence Worth Believing

Sometimes, talking about goals, dreams, and unmet desires can be triggering for people who have been told such aspirations are selfish. I grew up my whole life hearing that my heart was wicked, that what I wanted was suspect. But this is a terrible way to live. It's not really self-help if it's helping everyone except you. We need a system that acknowledges the reality of our pain and helps us deal with it.

Ultimately, your life is a story about you. Who else could it be about? It's your life, after all. You may believe your purpose here on Earth is to serve others and love them well, and that's wonderful. But who's doing the serving? Who's the one loving? You, of course. Your life is a narrative compiled of moments that make up your experience on planet Earth. And you are the main character. So let's make your story as good as possible.

This is an invitation to opt out of whatever matrix you're in and decide: *I know what's best for me. I see reality as best I can. I'm going to intentionally and attentively envision a better life for myself based on the reality of my life as I understand it right now.* Maybe, like me, you're tired of hearing "Just believe!" Or "Stay positive!" These platitudes don't work. What I'm offering, instead, is not an invitation to another methodology but rather an acknowledgment of how life already works. You've got everything you need to make the changes you want. Using persuasion to change your life works. It did for me.

Chapter 8

Making Yourself
Believe Anything

Alice laughed. "There's no use trying," she said. "One can't
believe impossible things."
"I daresay you haven't had much practice," said the Queen.
"When I was your age, I always did it for half-an-hour a
day. Why, sometimes I've believed as many as six impossible
things before breakfast."

—LEWIS CARROLL

W HEN I WAS SIXTEEN AND a Baptist, I was dating a girl who
belonged to the Church of Christ. There were a handful
of discrepancies between the way her church worshipped God and
the way mine did—namely, her church didn't believe in using mu-
sical instruments during services and mine did (although maybe
my church shouldn't have, if you know what I mean). However,
in the very religious culturescape of rural Tennessee, our dating

each other was like trying to mix oil with water. You kind of had to be there to understand, but the situation was the Southern version of the Capulets and Montagues. We were two star-crossed lovers, whose relationship would result in utter devastation for all involved. Aware of the chasm before us, she said we couldn't be together because we had very different belief systems—to which I replied, "Oh, that's okay. I can get myself to believe anything."

This was true then and is still (mostly) true today.

Ever since I was a little boy, I knew that the secret to creating any kind of change was convincing myself that something was true. I learned early on in life that to get what I wanted, I had to help someone see that it was true. This is called persuasion, and my natural fascination with this skill served me well as a marketer, copywriter, and entrepreneur. I have seen firsthand the power of changing people's minds, which can completely change their lives. So when it came to dating this girl I was really into, I didn't see a problem. I know, to some, it may seem that I was immoral or insincere, but I knew if I really dug into it, I would find things in this other belief system that I could get behind. So I did exactly that. I didn't believe all of what the Church of Christ held as true, but I didn't believe absolutely everything the Baptist Church had to say, either, so I figured it didn't matter too much. And I got a girlfriend out of changing my belief system.

One of the things that makes me good at what I do is that I am always open to new ideas and new information that could possibly change my mind about how I see the world. If there's something you want in life, and there are beliefs standing in your way, you have to find a way to convince yourself that there could be something true in a new way of looking at the world. We will cover this topic more in later sections of the book, but as we shed beliefs that no longer work for us, we will inevitably encounter what psychologists call "cognitive dissonance," which is a fancy name for what happens in your brain when the world as you experience it doesn't correspond to how you think it should be.

Put more simply, we feel bad when our expectations don't align with reality. As I've already shared, there is so much about the world that is unknowable, and belief itself is, in many ways, subjective. So why not find a way to convince yourself of a new belief system? If your old beliefs aren't working, then it's time to learn the art of persuasion. But before we do so, we have to grapple with the necessary tension we all experience when life doesn't unfold the way we believed it would.

Selling Myself on a Life That Didn't Suck

For years, I knew my beliefs weren't working, but I didn't know why. In this book, I've shared stories of the more problematic beliefs I've encountered in the "success industry," the Human Potential Movement, and even the hypercharismatic fundamentalist Christian community, but the truth is I wouldn't be here if I hadn't first been "brainwashed" by all these groups (among others). This understanding of how indoctrination works, both in a highly conservative religious environment and in the self-help personal development world, gave me the medicine that ultimately cured me—which is not what anyone expected, least of all me. I learned persuasion through these modalities of preachers and persuaders and then at the ripe old age of fifty decided: *Maybe I can believe whatever I want to believe. Maybe I can believe the way I see the world is actually accurate. I don't have to keep borrowing other people's filters for reality and keep trying to believe what they are telling me to believe. I can take belief as sort of an energy or a tool, and apply it in a way that works for me.*

Maybe we can believe whatever we want to believe. Maybe it's not about being able to know the "Truth" with a capital *T*. All answers to life's big questions, after all, are only approximations of the truth. These are our best guesses right now. Where do we go when we die? What's the meaning of life? How did we all get here? If you ask a scientist, a theologian, and an artist, you will get completely different answers, accompanied by some degree of certainty and conviction. If you challenge these ideas, you'll likely be met with some emotion (depending on whom you're talking with). That's a belief: an emotional connection to a thought that you think is true. And that's wonderful.

The goal here is not to find a convincing argument and commit to it forever; our understanding of the universe and how it works is always evolving, and we fill in the blanks of what we don't know with belief. Much of what we think is true is constantly being challenged and reconsidered. For about a hundred years, for instance, scientists believed atoms were irreducible; they were considered the most basic building block of the universe, and an atom couldn't be split. Today, we know that belief is not true, because we have devices that allow us to see subatomic particles and that can even split atoms. Beyond that, the field of string theory in physics is predicated on the idea that there is stuff smaller than atoms and electrons that holds everything together. And it is likely we are at least a little wrong, which is to say there's always more to learn.

So when we persuade ourselves to believe whatever we want, this is not some capricious quest to jump onto the latest conspiracy-theory bandwagon. On the contrary, it is a rigorous process of trying ideas on and seeing how they fit your life. The goal is to have beliefs you want to have, not just ones that have been thrust upon you, because what you believe in many ways determines how you behave and therefore how you live. The quality of your beliefs, not the veracity of them, is what makes your life meaningful; whether the belief is entirely true doesn't matter as much as how deep your convictions go.

How do you build better beliefs? You test them—run them through the mill of your own doubts and questions to see how reliable they are. No one wants to believe something that they don't really think is true. We all know people in various religions and cultures who sort of believe a thing because they're supposed to or because they'll get in trouble if they don't. People who live that way are often not very happy; I know, because I lived that way for a very long time. So again, I say: the goal here is to have beliefs you want to have, beliefs that work for you—*durable* beliefs, ones that can withstand the storms of life.

We need to grow up in our beliefs, not in terms of what we believe but how. Remember, the goal of self-help, after all, is to help yourself. The idea is for you to be in charge, not somebody else. There's nothing wrong with trusting a teacher. But when we blindly follow someone, accepting what they say without questioning or needing to verify it, we are giving away the one thing that we mustn't give away, which is our own personal power. We can't become our best selves if we're stuck trying to satisfy the whims of someone else, no matter how persuasive or charismatic that person may be.

What I humbly hope to do, in part, through this book is to bring these communities back to their original intentions. Every one of these organizations or companies has a book or manifesto—a document of persuasion. When Tony Robbins's *Awaken the Giant Within* came out in 1991, I discovered that it was the foundational material that was in his expensive seminars. The book is a long advertisement for his live training.

I wonder if we can say such a thing about the Bible. I think we can, without disrespecting it or denigrating it. It is a document.

The most ardent fundamentalist will tell you that if this is the document by which you live, you will advance in the kingdom of God. This document is intended to change your belief systems and structures and to get them to line up with what believers in the Bible feel is the correct set of beliefs and practices to improve your life. By its very nature and by its own claims, the Bible is the ultimate self-help book.

I know a lot of Christians will take issue with that statement, responding, "It's not about you." But of course it is about me, because who am I trying to save from burning in hell? Me! We want our lives to be better and our afterlives to be better, too—a little less crispy, if you will; 100 percent not deep-fried. And in that respect, the Bible works quite well.

There was a time in my radio career when I realized that whenever I was taking a position and advocating for something within the company, I needed to write a document that persuaded my coworkers. I needed to write a sales letter. They didn't know that, but I had read Jay Abraham's work on sales letters and was familiar with the work of Claude Hopkins by this time, as well. I wrote a "white paper" to sell the company on the idea of having an internet division. It worked, and the internet division of the company was ultimately sold for tens of millions of dollars.

That's when I started writing sales letters for myself every year about what I wanted to achieve in the next year. I wrote a letter about my goals to sell myself on what I wanted to achieve. It was early in my radio career that I realized, *I'm going to write this persuasive document to myself, to get myself to do the things I know I should do anyway.* That's what this book is, too: a sales letter for me, just as much as it is for anyone else—to remind us all to keep choosing our own power and belief system.

That's what we'll be working on in this next part, learning the fundamental steps of writing a great sales letter and turning that persuasive power on yourself.

Read This or Die

You saw earlier the sales letter I wrote to myself when I realized I needed to wake up and take my last chance before it expired. I titled it "The Most Important Sales Letter You'll Ever Read" because it was written to me—and if I didn't have me, I wouldn't have anything else. I'm a proponent of keeping myself around for as long as possible. I'm sure you are, too. Here are the components that you saw in my letter and that should be in yours:

+ **The callout.** This is written directly to the person to whom it needs to go. In this case, me. And in your case, you.

+ **The headline.** I based this on a headline ("Read This or Die!") written by a good friend of mine who passed away a few years ago. I feel as though he's participated in helping me write the most important sales letter ever for myself, and that makes it all the more meaningful.

+ **Calling out a specific thing to change.** This grabs my attention. There is something that needs to change, and I know what it is.

+ **Imagery.** A great visual goes a long way, especially when you're drawing the image of *bleeding regret*.

+ **A question.** I ask myself, "Why did you wait until now?" To any reader, this would be the next logical question. I'm writing directly to the pain. Ask yourself the question you have been avoiding.

+ **Marketing mind reading.** In my letter, I wrote, "Here are the lions, crouched outside your door, waiting to see whether you will let them eat you alive." My Christian upbringing is so deeply rooted in my psyche that this sentence conjures an image of myself facing a choice: to fight with the army of God or the army of Satan. When you actually *can* read the mind of your prospect (and the only time you can do so is when the prospect is you), then you already know what to say! Be bold and compassionate—write what moves you.

+ **Bold words.** Bold words draw the eye across the copy.

+ **Presenting a future picture of paradise.** Show the reader (again, *you*) what will happen if you do the following action. Build a story you wish to enter and live in.

+ **Call to action.** If I'm up for the challenge, this tells me what to do now.

DO THIS

Take the components I just explained to you from the letter I wrote myself and take a stab at writing your own letter. Don't worry about "getting it right." It's more important that you simply get it written. We can clean it up later. The goal is to get words down first. Remember that this is life-changing stuff here, when done the right way. More than the eloquence of the words is the emotion behind them. That's what changes you: how you feel when writing and reading this letter.

Chapter 9

Reinforcing New Realities

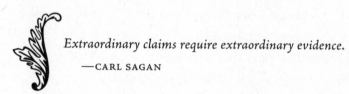 *Extraordinary claims require extraordinary evidence.*
—CARL SAGAN

ABOUT A MONTH AFTER MY Parkinson's diagnosis, I went to talk to my neurologist about the ketogenic diet. This was about ten years ago, so "keto" was not as popular as it is today. One of the only places you could hear about it was on the podcast of Tim Ferriss, who mentioned that the diet was used to treat epileptic children who had not responded to medication. He also wrote briefly about the diet on his blog and in his book *The 4-Hour Body*. That was interesting to me, because it seemed there was some sort of neurological link there.

As I began doing more research, I discovered the powerful effect of MCT (medium-chain triglyceride) oil and how it related to a ketogenic diet, in which your body burns ketones instead of sugar. Burning ketones rather than sugar is better for your brain; it elevates brain function and BDNF (brain-derived neurotrophic factor), which is like fertilizer that neurons grow in. I began discovering all this evidence that there were things I could do to alter the course of my disease and maybe even reverse the symptoms. I found a number of people who had experienced a reversal of their symptoms by eating keto and doing regular, intense exercise. That was enough to give me hope.

I took all this information to my neurologist, and he said, "That's fringe stuff. It's hard on your body. Don't do it." So I didn't talk to him about it anymore, but meanwhile began both the keto diet and regular exercise. During a visit with him one day about five years later, my neurologist told me, "Hey, I don't know if you've seen this. There's a study that says eating a ketogenic diet might be helpful. Have you considered that?" I told him I had already been following that diet for about five years. He laughed. We have a pretty fun relationship; I think I drove him crazy at first, but we've come to be good friends, and he's very open now when I bring in my ideas I've read about somewhere on Dr. Google. These days, he asks whether I've heard of a particular treatment or a particular protocol and whether I might want to try it. We're always working together on things like that.

This is a process that is never-ending. If you are facing a situation or challenge that is chronic, that is with you for a long time, this process goes on forever. Even cancer patients who respond to treatment and who can now say "I'm cancer-free!" still know it's not over. Most still have to keep going back year after year to get tested and assessed to make sure the cancer doesn't come back. There's always that fear that the cancer is still there but lying dormant; it could come back at some point. For anybody who's dealing with a chronic illness or chronic problem, it's useful to continuously be updating your evidentiary database. You have to keep building your case.

The next step in believing a new reality is creating a preponderance of evidence and witnessing a transformation. To have hope that things can be different for you, you need to see someone else living out that different way of being. If you want to alter the story you're living, begin with other people's stories. The easiest way to believe in a new reality is to see someone else already living it. Before you can lose the weight, you might need to see a friend lose it. Before you can be happy in your relationship, you might need to see another couple completely in love. This intentional cognitive bias requires you to look for ways of solving your problem by paying attention to those who have already solved the same problem. Educate yourself as much as you can on all the different belief systems related to solving your problem.

When people purchase the P90X workout program, they aren't simply buying a program with DVDs, charts, and so on. Of course, those are the mechanisms through which people will achieve change. But what they are actually purchasing is that lean, healthy, youthful physique they saw in the commercials—the transformation they saw someone else have, in the before-and-after pictures—and now believe is possible for themselves.

I received my hope for transformation from an unlikely source: Beethoven. He wrote close to 130 pieces of music, only 30 of them before he went deaf as a child. He had actually written a suicide note to his brothers that they found locked in a desk, decades after his death, in which he wrote about how angry he was: "Why would God give me the gift of music and then rob me of my hearing?" People hear *Moonlight Sonata* and think it's so peaceful, but it's not about peace; it's really about anger. Beethoven wrote that piece out of fury. In fact, he ended up writing all his best works after he went deaf, in spite of (or perhaps because of) that great challenge.

Helen Keller and Stephen Hawking are others I look to and

think, *Would they have created their greatest work if they had not been faced with such adversity?* I don't think so. I don't think they would have been driven to do so. How much worse would our world be without these people's contributions? And what would their contributions be without the adversity? Your inspiration for transformation does not have to come from infomercials or historical figures. Maybe you just need to see two people truly in love to believe romance is possible. Maybe you just need to meet one person who started their own business to believe you can, too. Search for those stories, and let them reshape your reality.

The Brain Is an Artifact for Life

All of your emotions, sensations, and experiences add up to give you the personality you have today. Your brain is a record of all those experiences; it is an artifact of your life. Dr. Joe Dispenza calls the brain a record of the past. In many ways, our brain and personality are really the sum total of our experiences; they tell us what has been true and can help us predict only futures that are in line with our experiences thus far. Most of us don't take the time to even think about this fact. Most of us did not consciously choose the conclusions, beliefs, and rules upon which we've built our entire philosophy of living. These were taught to us piecemeal; in many ways, we "caught" our philosophy of life from our parents, teachers, and other influences.

At the age of fifteen, twenty, or thirty, most people do not sit down and say to themselves, "I'm going to think about my philosophy of life. And I'm going to have an organized system of thinking about life." But we all have a philosophy, whether we realize it or not. In her book *Philosophy: Who Needs It*, Ayn Rand wrote:

As a human being, you have no choice about the fact that you need a philosophy. Your only choice is whether you define your philosophy by a conscious, rational, disciplined process of thought and scrupulously logical deliberation—or let your subconscious accumulate a junk heap of unwarranted conclusions, false generalizations, undefined contradictions, undigested slogans, unidentified wishes, doubts and fears, thrown together by chance, but integrated by your subconscious into a kind of mongrel philosophy and fused into a single, solid weight: self-doubt, like a ball and chain in the place where your mind's wings should have grown.

If the brain is a record of your past, an artifact of you, as it were, your habituated emotional patterns are a part of this artifact. Ninety percent of your daily thoughts are the same thoughts you had the day before. In my experience, most of the thoughts I have today are the same thoughts I had yesterday. This is practicing what Dr. Joe Dispenza calls "the habit of being yourself." If you want to change the results you're getting in your life, you have to stop being the same person. Your body becomes the record of your present past mind and your present past thoughts. If you want to become a different body and have a different experience in the world, then you've got to reprogram your body with a mind that looks to the future. In other words, you've got to stop thinking the same thoughts, which can be quite hard.

We are used to believing a certain thing, not necessarily knowing where that belief came from. If we grew up believing one political party was the enemy, then we have unconsciously looked for patterns to prove that belief is true. Our minds don't like being wrong, so we search for reasons to be right. Consider the religion you belong to, a social group with which you identify, or even a moral idea you believe is true (for example, "Abortion is murder" or "Health care should be free"); then imagine someone challenges the veracity of that idea.

What do you do? What have you done in the past?

If you're like most people, you defend your position. Sure, maybe you externally listen to the other side in the name of being "open-minded," but aren't you silently reminding yourself why you're right and the other person is wrong? Can you notice your mind searching for evidence to prove that your position is, in fact, correct? There's nothing wrong with this tendency; it's quite normal and natural, nothing to be ashamed of. This psychological phenomenon is called "cognitive bias" and explains why, even when faced with data that could cause them to doubt their position on a matter, most people tend to argue with the arguments and double down on their belief systems.

It is only in the face of an overwhelming amount of evidence that a person will actually change their mind, admit they were wrong, and be open to believing something else. When dealing with Parkinson's, I knew I had certain biases of which I was unaware—belief systems that in some ways were keeping me stuck in my suffering. But, I wondered, could I use this form of brainwashing on myself to help me change my mind for the better, to get me to believe something that might make my life much easier? And if I could, how would I go about it? Well, I am not easy to convince; so I would certainly need a lot of evidence.

A Preponderance of Proof

Dan Kennedy wrote in No B.S. Sales Success in the New Economy, "Having a preponderance of proof makes it possible to sell with 100 percent effectiveness, 100 percent of the time. If you want to win with every presentation of every proposition, make sure you have an overwhelming amount of proof that what you are selling is a great deal, have an overwhelming quality of proof, and have proof that is influential." I remember him giving a talk once in which he said that however much proof you think you need to convince somebody—and he was talking about marketing and sales—try piling on ten times as much as you think you need, and really overdo it.

I took that advice to heart in my business affairs, offering case studies and testimonials galore in every sales letter I wrote. And it worked—like a charm, in fact. Many of my friends and peers began calling on me to help them with their own sales letters, and I did. Almost always, their sales were lacking because they were not offering a "preponderance of proof." They thought it was enough to provide one or two examples of success—it wasn't. Because of people's cognitive biases, you really have to go over the top to persuade them. And I realized that if that technique works in sales letters, it might also work in life, especially when it comes to changing one's beliefs.

As I mentioned, I've studied the work of Tony Robbins for a very long time, and one of his core teachings is the analogy of the table: belief is the tabletop, and the legs are the evidence supporting it. The whole premise is that you need to come up with enough evidence (that is, legs) to convince yourself this thing is true. As I considered this idea, I discovered that without realizing it, I had done this very thing, not only in my copywriting and marketing, but in my life. When I would go to a self-improvement seminar or learn from some teacher, I would stock up on all their books, courses, and other material. I wanted to make sure I indoctrinated myself into whatever belief they were pitching, so that I really believed it fully.

I wanted the transformation these people were selling, so I'd go in search of ways for it to be true. This is what I call an "intentional cognitive bias," which is a way of essentially convincing yourself something is true by gathering enough data to change your view on a matter. We sometimes do so unconsciously, but I want to encourage you to do so consciously, in a way that leads you in a direction that will make your life better.

This intentional cognitive bias requires you to look for new ways of solving your problem by paying attention to those who have already solved the problem. This is the same principle as getting a "preponderance of proof" so that you can believe that what you're doing will actually have an effect. It's also known as the placebo effect. In his book *You Are the Placebo: Making Your Mind Matter*, Dispenza tells the story of Parkinson's patients who received deep brain stimulation surgery. In this surgery, doctors drill holes in your head and run wires into your brain. They stimulate deep areas of your brain with electromagnetic signals that cancel out the tremor and movement part of the disorder. It seems to me to be a very barbaric surgery, but a lot of Parkinson's patients have it because they feel they've run out of options. In the book, Dispenza relates that researchers did a study in which some of the patients received a "sham surgery." Doctors actually made the incisions and put the patients under anesthesia but did not insert the wires. Those patients had the same result as the patients who had the actual procedure. When the researchers finally told the study subjects what had really happened, more than half of them still retained the positive result.

Reading about this was a huge "WTF?" moment. One of the things Dispenza is doing now is tracking the results of the people who attend his workshops, looking for the epigenetic changes that result from the practices he teaches. Participants in his workshops do a lot of deep, mindful meditation—or, as I like to think of it, reprogramming their brains with new language. Alan Watts gave a talk about words and how they shape our worldview. If we don't have words for something, then we don't have a lot of the problems that come with those words. Rather, we just have the experience of the moment.

We have to stop that endless thought loop in our head that elevates our cortisol levels and activates our fight-or-flight response. Being in that condition continuously puts the body in a state of depleted energy, depleted immune response, and depleted resources. When you stay in panic mode long enough, you can't think well. So now you're making poor choices, and it's a habit that's wreaking havoc on your body. If you can put yourself in a state of mind in which you are thinking in ways that bring you calm and peace, you can begin to recover. Some people miraculously completely recover, and others can at least ameliorate their symptoms. They can have a better experience of life. For me, there's enough evidence that our thoughts affect the quality of our lives.

Building Your Own World

When I decided my beliefs weren't working, it wasn't a simple flip of the switch to change from one set of biases to another. You can't just change your beliefs willy-nilly. You can pretend to believe something, but at the end of the day, when push comes to shove, what you truly believe will come out.

I had changed my beliefs my whole life in various ways. When I changed what I thought about money and work, my income went up. When I changed my beliefs about success, I started selling more products and building a better life for myself. But none of it was natural. My inclination was always to hide, to stay stuck in my old ways of being. These ways were, after all, habitual; I was well practiced in the art of being myself. So, I had to make an intentional change. Doing so took time, focus, and a lot of evidence.

If you decide on what you want out of life, you have to first determine what beliefs are needed to get you there. No wishful thinking will help you. What evidence is required for you to believe those beliefs? We can't be like Stuart Smalley, simply repeating to ourselves in the mirror, "I'm good enough, I'm smart enough, and doggone it, people like me!" That doesn't work; trust me, I tried it for years. Making a statement without the evidence to back it up won't result in changing your thinking about a damn thing. And if your thoughts don't change, your life won't, either. Practice your belief until you perfect it.

Sometimes I would want to accumulate the evidence, but it wasn't there. Then I'd have to choose a different belief. Remember: the belief is the tabletop, and the evidence is the legs. If there are no legs, there is no table. You've got to remain open and humble, willing to be wrong, so that you can find a better belief. The key is asking yourself, "What does this make possible? What changes will it make if I believe it?" You have to believe there's enough benefit, because it is a pain to change. You will experience unpleasant withdrawal symptoms, breaking free of your old beliefs. But this is how we change and grow and heal.

In terms of Parkinson's, the medical community at large says it is incurable. They say there's no "disease-altering treatment," only "symptom-ameliorating treatment." That belief wasn't useful to me, so I went looking for people who had been cured, who had experienced a remission or complete reversal. There were lots of people who had experienced such things. It took time to accumulate this evidence, but slowly I began to see that another way of living just might be possible. That's when I started my ketogenic diet, years before my doctor acknowledged that it could be helpful.

As I began looking for evidence to prove what I wanted to believe, I kept all my notes and documents on my computer, assembled in one app. I set up reminders on all my devices to review these materials on a regular basis, dragging them out and reviewing each one periodically. This was my version of reciting affirmations: reviewing the "preponderance of proof" I was assembling for what I wanted to be true.

I still review these materials regularly. This review of evidence always leads me to wonder what new information there might be out there. For example, I'll be reading something Dr. Rhonda Patrick said four years ago and think, *I wonder if she's got any new information.* Then I'll go chase down any new materials or resources she might have, or I'll go to a handful of reliable medical websites and look for any new studies. I do this quarterly, but if I'm feeling particularly frustrated or confused, I sometimes do it daily. Or I'll talk to my neurologist, Dr. Greeley, and say, "Hey, what's the latest you hear? What's the newest cutting-edge thing?" We have a great relationship where we both trust each other's ideas and opinions. I've also got a network of friends who alert me to new breakthrough studies and treatments. I used to isolate myself from the Parkinson's community at large, because I didn't want to be around old, shaky people. Now, I find it helpful to be around other people with Parkinson's, and I also want to help teach them because doing so helps reinforce my own beliefs.

As a lover of science fiction and fantasy novels, I appreciate that one of their writers' key practices is the construction of a whole society, magic system, or scientific system of knowledge—which they call "world building." A key part of world building is making sure the system you're constructing is consistent. It has to be built with integrity—with consistent beliefs, structures, and premises. World building is what I'm doing when I'm writing a sales letter. I'm building a new world for myself, or for the client.

In this new world, we see things differently. We're changing our beliefs, and we're building a whole new philosophy. As Ayn Rand once remarked, I am always in the process of consciously defining and refining my view toward life. If you don't have a philosophy for the world you're creating, it's not going to hold together. And the world beyond your control will give you one.

Challenging Authority

Many of us are programmed to think that there are certain authorities who have answers. What we call an "authority" is basically someone who has a belief attached to a lot of evidence. When I first started seeing my neurologist, I viewed him as a godlike authority. But as I challenged him and continued to bring evidence to the table, he changed some of his views. I've had similar experiences with other specialists and authorities, challenging some of their most closely held beliefs. And I've seen these intelligent, well-educated experts shift their positions because of what I've said. Yes, it's wise to trust the body of research available to us, but these are not facts; they are only ideas, things people think are true. And sometimes, even doctors can be wrong. And I, too, can be terribly incorrect about something I was certain about. The same is true for us all.

Here's the rub, though: nobody is the authority on your life but you. As Ralph Waldo Emerson wrote, "Nothing is at last sacred but the integrity of your own mind." There's no such thing as someone who's right or wrong when it comes to belief. There are just people who have ideas that are attached to a certain body of evidence. And for almost every belief, you can find a set of so-called facts proving it wrong. It's important to understand this idea, because people capitulate way too quickly to authorities and let them control their lives. I always think of what Upton Sinclair wrote, that it is difficult to get a man to understand something when his salary depends upon his not understanding it—for example, telling a doctor that a certain kind of medication doesn't work. But this is your life we are talking about; you can't afford to believe someone else who might be wrong. Test the ideas, find your own evidence, and choose beliefs that work for you.

In a way, the same human nature that leads people to think the earth is six thousand years old or that the sun revolves around the earth also leads us to think that new neurons can never be formed in the brain or that diet can't have an effect on an incurable disease. These are just ideas that may or may not be true; but when we believe them, they may become true.

So, then, we have to be courageous enough to become our own authorities, despite what the rest of the pack may say. Yes, we can test things out and have our "peer reviews," but we cannot abdicate the responsibility of belief to anyone else. Being your own authority is always hard for humans, whether we are scientists or preachers. Before the change arrives, first comes the evidence; after that, we have the opportunity to live out a whole new story for real.

DO THIS

In what areas of your life have you abdicated responsibility for deciding what is true? What areas of your life do you need to take command of? What are some ideas you never decided to accept, but rather simply accept them? How can you challenge those ideas, or test those that are in opposition? You know what to do: *Write!*

PART V

Opportunity—The Invitation to Change

Why do we not get what we want out of life? Because of what we believe. Many of us have been taught to think of our beliefs as fixed ideas about the way the universe works, such as a belief in gravity, but that's not true. Beliefs change all the time. Understanding this is key to our happiness and success. As a marketer, I am trained in the art of persuasion. Every day, I help people change their beliefs, often without their realizing it. If that sounds a little dastardly, that's because it is—or at least it can be.

Marketing, especially the kind I was trained in, is designed to subvert a person's rational thinking and get them to emotionally agree to something, then use reason to rationalize the decision. This is the way much of our society works, from the politicians we elect to the type of fabric softener we buy. We think these decisions are ours, but very often, they are not. They are psychologically preprogrammed ahead of time and then implanted in us, like a microchip, so that when the time comes, we respond appropriately.

Would you believe me if I told you it was possible to change what you believe? You might not, but that's just another belief. And trust me, I can change it—or rather, I can help you create the conditions under which you will change what you believe. As someone who has been trained in the dark arts of manipulation, I am sorry to say your beliefs are far from objective observations about what's real in the world. Your beliefs are a mix of ideas inherited from your parents, society, religion, and political party, along with several other people or influential moments in time. What we believe comes from other people and is reinforced by the emotional nature of our own experience.

There's nothing wrong with belief, of course; it's how we navigate the mysteries of life. What happens, though, when your way of seeing the world no longer aligns with what you experience?

For me, a diagnosis of Parkinson's disease forced me to acknowledge the brokenness of my own beliefs and sent me on an existential journey that was confusing, frightening, and ultimately enlightening. On this journey, I broke down the very concept of belief and began to view it not as a fixed way of seeing the world but as a useful tool for motivating myself and others. What I had previously believed about life no longer matched my experience. This disconnect left me feeling a little crazy. Ultimately, I had to make a decision: double down on what wasn't working or change what I believed before my beliefs broke me for good.

Chapter 10

Calling Yourself to Action

It is important that you get clear for yourself that your only access to impacting life is action. The world does not care what you intend, how committed you are, how you feel or what you think, and certainly it has no interest in what you want and don't want. Take a look at life as it is lived and see for yourself that the world only moves for you when you act.

—WERNER ERHARD

THIRTY YEARS AGO, WHEN I was working in radio, I would often tell my staff of disc jockeys, "Look, if we do this, we'll boost business and get great ratings. If you go out and meet and greet people, get to know them, do direct mail, make a certain number of appearances, position our radio station in this way, we'll make more money, which will lead to you getting bonuses and being happier in your career."

Simple, right? If they followed my instructions, they'd make more money and therefore be happier. Seems logical, yes? Too bad they didn't do it. This baffled me. I was giving them the keys to a fulfilling and successful career, and no one wanted to listen to me. To fix this problem, our station hired a top radio consultant to advise me on running the station. His name was Bob, and he asked me, "Why do you believe this should work?"

"Because," I said, "if I explain to people how to get what they want, they should just do it." *I mean, how hard is this, people?!*

"But," Bob said, "that's not working. Would you rather have what you feel is an accurate belief about what works, or would you rather have a useful belief?"

I said, "I'd rather have an accurate belief." He asked why, and I said, "Because I'm right." It always feels good to be right, doesn't it?

"Well," Bob rephrased, "would you rather be right or would you rather have a job?"

Hmm, good point, I thought and finally came around: "Okay, we'll try it your way."

We ended up giving out more emotional rewards, such as personal attention, recognition, and affirmation that the employees were valuable members of the team. I started taking people out to lunch and spending more time with each of them, asking them, "What's important to you? What really makes you happy?"

One guy told me, "I just want a truck. I want a *big* truck."

"Why?" I asked.

"Because it makes me feel like I'm a real man."

This man and I talked about trucks, cars, and motorcycles and about love for the outdoors. We worked out a trade with a Ford dealership: he did live-read ads about their trucks and in return got his truck. He was happier than I'd ever seen him, all because of a truck. Of course, it wasn't about the truck. It was about figuring out what he wanted (and why he wanted it).

That, my friend, is everything. Getting higher ratings and bonuses was what *I* wanted but not what my team wanted. I was trying to motivate them based on my own desires, and that never works.

What Is Life Like?

Behind every goal is a motivation, and guiding that motivation is a belief in what this accomplishment will make possible for us. Many people are out of touch with their motivation or simply do not trust it, relegating it to the same category as self-help clichés and positive-thinking aphorisms. In many cases, we who have been burned by this word set our sights on some big change only to experience failure and feel a sense of disappointment after not getting what we wanted. As disillusioned as we may be, though, the truth is we can't create change without motivation. What motivates you reveals what you believe is possible. Before you can put your desired change into effect, then, you must tap into what motivates you.

And this may, in fact, surprise you.

How do you know what your motivations are? Pay attention. Most marketers are aware of the power of stories to get people to take action. And as a seasoned copywriter whose job is to motivate people to take action, I love a good metaphor. They're simple and straightforward, and most people get them right away. Metaphors work, especially when it comes to persuading people. Moreover, all of Joseph Campbell's work can be summarized this way: for thousands of years, human beings have told myths to help them make meaning out of the mystery of existence. In fact, Campbell has even called God a metaphor for something much deeper and more complex and beautiful than we can imagine. I love that.

If you pay close enough attention to many of the stories that have been repeated over and over again, across cultures and centuries, you start to see certain characteristics emerging that almost all human beings seem to possess. This is the way we understand others, by first understanding and examining ourselves. Before we can persuade others, we first have to discover what motivates us. And that starts with a story. We all love the triumph of a hero over a villain. We see this, of course, in comedies, stories that result in a happy ending; we also see the same value reflected in tragedies. Nobody feels good at the end of *Macbeth*, and that's the point. These stories reveal to us the nature of humanity, of what we want to happen—that is, our true motivations.

So if you're struggling to know what motivates you, pay attention to your global metaphors and beliefs, your responses about why things happen the way they do. For example, let's say a friend of yours was recently dumped by their significant other, and your friend is heartbroken. But you respond somewhat glibly, "Nothing lasts forever." Maybe you didn't even think about what you were saying; you just blurted it out. That's a global belief. Such beliefs tend to run our lives without our realizing it. But sometimes, those can be rather difficult to uncover. It's usually easier to find a global metaphor than it is to find a global belief. So let's start there.

Ask yourself quickly, without thinking too much, "What is life like if you had to describe it?" This is your global metaphor. Global metaphors are our way of masking what we truly believe, giving a surface appearance to how we see the world. For example, if I said to you, "Life is a game," that's a global metaphor. It gives you a sense of what I really believe, how I see the world, and will even give you a sense of what motivates me. Conversely, if I said, "Life is a battle," or "Life is a fight," this would reveal something entirely different. Wouldn't it?

I have a friend who says life is "trial by fire," which certainly reveals a lot about how he sees the world, what he believes is possible, and ultimately what motivates him. You can find your global metaphor a lot faster than your global beliefs. If my global metaphor is "Life is a battlefield," what beliefs could lie underneath that? Who's the battle with? Is it a battle of good versus evil? Whose side are you on? Are you a soldier, a general, a bystander? All kinds of beliefs could be behind that metaphor. If your first response is "Life is a beautiful gift," you're operating with an entirely different set of beliefs from someone who says, "Life is heartache."

Once we have a sense of our global metaphor, then we know what we're working with. This metaphor also tends to reveal your global beliefs. You don't have to stay stuck here, but you always have to start with where you are, with what you believe and what you think is possible. Once you understand where you're coming from, you can reshape where you're going.

A useful practice is to ask, "What kind of person do I want to be? And what is that person's global metaphor? What are that person's global beliefs?" If a person believes life is a beautiful gift, then the person also probably believes there's a giver and a receiver. They likely have beliefs about what their mission is—maybe to pass on the gifts, or maybe to accept gifts with joy and gratitude.

Change comes down to deciding what kind of person you want to be like and then becoming like that person. To be who you want to be, start with how you see the world and what your global metaphors are, and then reimagine your perspective. You can choose to be the tragic victim or the triumphant hero. You could even be the villain or a bystander. Who do you want to be? What global metaphor will guide your life, and what beliefs will inform how you show up in this story? Take the advice of one who played the victim for many years, and choose to be the hero. You may have to dismantle a bunch of broken beliefs and become a completely different person along the way (I did), but it'll be worth it. Before you do that, though, you may have to get a little more honest.

Telling the Truth About What Motivates You

The worst thing that can happen to a person is that they succeed too early and without the maturity to know what to do with success. As an ambitious person who has surrounded himself with high performers for most of my life, I've seen this cycle repeated over and over again. When a person succeeds, they get the thing that they think they wanted, and it rarely satisfies them. But when you see how relatively easy it is to get something you want, this can lead to a whole life of chasing things that ultimately don't make you happy. I've followed this path, and it led me into a hole that was hard to climb out of. The reason I felt so dissatisfied for most of my life was because I told myself that I was doing things for my family or for God or for the people I wanted to help. And there's some truth to that, but it wasn't the whole truth.

Recently, I overheard a conversation between a couple of successful men. One of them asked the other, "Who are you doing this for?"

The other man responded, "I know what the 'right' answer is. The right answer is for my little girl and wife. But the truth is I'm doing it for me . . . I'm the most important person to me."

The reason people succeed is because they want to, because they have an innately selfish desire to accomplish something. I'm not here to tell you that's right or wrong; but as a marketer, I know the most important part of my job is to speak honestly to my potential customer. If I don't, they won't listen to me. They won't trust me, because human beings can usually tell when other people are lying. If we are going to persuade ourselves of anything, we must be honest about what actually motivates us.

This is hard to admit. I come from a faith tradition that says selfishness is sin and the root of all that's wrong with the world. Certainly, there's some truth to that. One of the things that makes humanity great is our ability to cooperate with one another, to trade and barter, and sometimes to give up what we want for the sake of the greater good. And yet, I know, as a trained persuader, that most people are motivated to act out of their own self-interest. This is the secret to selling anyone anything: find out what a person really wants and offer them a believable way to get it.

As anyone in my field who's worth their salt will tell you, people are rarely honest about what they want. The conversation of the two men I overheard was like a breath of fresh air, because I had had those thoughts before and dismissed them, repressed them. The man wasn't saying that his motivation was right or good, just that it was there. And that's honest. I can respect that. An honest person is one who can persuade—and be persuaded. We must tell the truth to ourselves, at least, if we want to change things. The point is not to have the right motivation, but to know what yours is.

What motivates you? I mean, really. Is it a big truck? A special place in heaven? A happy life? Sex, food, fun? You don't have to be honest with me or your spouse or even your neighbor about your motivation (I accept no responsibility for any marital issues this advice may incur). But if you can't admit what you want at least to yourself, you won't be able to get it—ever. You can't change if you aren't honest. You'll keep believing the same broken beliefs, causing you to suffer and feel stifled.

In the New Testament, Jesus asks a man whether he wants to be healed, to which the man replies, "I believe! Help my unbelief." That's honest. We can work with that. If you want to believe something other than what you've believed—maybe that life can be beautiful, that you can be successful, or that something hard can be easy—then you have to start with motivation, which means you've got to reckon with yourself about what you really want. If you say you want something, but then find out the pursuit of that something is going to make your life incredibly difficult, and you don't want that difficulty, then you don't want to pursue that thing. At least, you don't want to badly enough to endure the hardship it'll take. That's fine; that's wonderful, in fact. This is you realizing you don't really want that thing—a realization that is freeing.

There comes a point in life when you may not have the emotional fuel you need to push yourself over how hard it's going to be to get the thing you wanted. So you give up and say, "Oh well, it's not worth it to me." You might phrase it that way in your head. This happens to a lot of people. It's normal. And this is the point where we can use belief to motivate us, to tap into what truly matters to us, and then to allow us to reshape our worldview in a way that results in true and lasting transformation. After all, motivation is just another kind of belief.

Finding a Why That Works

All change is guided by motivation; and you cannot motivate anyone without tapping into the power of belief. The kind of motivation I'm talking about is not the kind that has you jumping on a chair and chanting affirmations at the top of your lungs. When I say motivation, I mean the kind that comes with accountability and action, the kind that leads to true and lasting change, not just a weekend high from a twelve-hour seminar.

In copywriting, we use the audience's motivation to call them to action. Motivation is not a feeling so much as a habit. The word simply means "a motive for action." What is your motive for action? Why do you eat the things you say you don't want to eat, which give you results that you don't want to have? Yet you keep eating those things. The thing you think is your motivation is not really your motivation. What really motivates you is the thought *I like the way it feels when I eat the apple pie.* Maybe you link eating the apple pie with feeling loved or cared for or comforted. That's fine, no judgment. For years, I ate all kinds of sweets, because I associated those foods with comfort. But after a while, that belief no longer worked; I hated how those foods made me feel. I needed a new motivation, one that was more helpful, one that I could believe.

After my Parkinson's diagnosis, I had a decision to make. I could sit in the unbearable pain of my belief, or I could find out what was really motivating me and try to find something better to believe. Previously, my belief in positive thinking and healing prayers had helped me level up in life, but now it was preventing me from getting what I wanted, which was peace and happiness. I needed to believe something new. To paraphrase Nietzsche, I could endure any obstacle I faced if I had a reason to do so. I believed that—mostly—and I wanted to figure out what my *why* was now that my world had been turned upside down.

But was I willing to do the work?

My priorities are: first, my relationship with God; and second, the stewardship and care of my own life. I use the word "God," but I am comfortable with words such as "Source" and "Universe" and even "Energy." What I do know—after much experimentation that is still ongoing—is my life is more fulfilling when it feels connected to a mysterious and divine source. Life is a gift. My consciousness is a gift. How do I best care for those gifts? I take care of them. These days, I'm a pretty good steward of my life. I work out, eat well, try to get good rest (though my condition sometimes prevents me from doing so), and do my best to reach my potential. Why? Because it feels good, and I believe this is my right and responsibility as a human being.

Life becomes meaningful only in relationship with other people. Existence, in my experience, is more enjoyable when I spend a good chunk of time giving my talents to others after first giving them to myself. I am the most important person in my universe. After that priority come the relationships I have with my wife, my son, and my other family members and friends. These are the right priorities, in my opinion. I don't know whether this is true for everybody, but it works for me right now. Maybe later, it won't. I don't know. Beliefs don't change that often for me—rather, they evolve after time in the same way that scientific theories are always undergoing evolution and slowly changing from one form into another. Someday, I may believe differently. But for now, this works.

DO THIS

It's a dandy idea to live a "purpose-driven life," but what *is* your purpose? You get to decide. Try asking and answering that question on paper, right now: "What is my purpose for living? What's most important to me?" After this question comes the follow-up inquiry: "And why is it so important?" Ask that question several more times of each successive answer you come up with. In our workshops, we do this seven times, and we call the exercise "Seven Levels Deep." If you get seven levels deep into this question and exploration, you're going to have a much clearer answer as to what your purpose really is.

Chapter 11

Closing the Deal

 When we are no longer able to change a situation ...
we are challenged to change ourselves.
—VIKTOR FRANKL

THE RESPONSE STEP (R) OF the PASTOR method is when you
just *do* it. It's also the time that you find a way to be accountable
and put yourself in situations where you're likely to follow through.
Once you have the plan, it's time to respond. How do you get moving? By giving yourself an incentive to start now instead of later. By
giving yourself consequences for not taking action and rewards for
starting. By reminding yourself that this new way of living is better
than what you were doing before. To persuade anyone—including
ourselves—of anything, we've got to learn how to close the deal.

Consequences close. The higher the stakes, the more seriously
we take the situation. So when it comes to motivating ourselves into
uncomfortable action, we may have to get creative. This might mean

making a bet with a friend or giving yourself a certain "prize" when you take a step in the right direction. It could mean surrounding yourself with a community that will encourage your new choices. Whatever route you take, you will have to retrain your brain to associate this new activity with something positive.

When I write a sales letter, at this point I really want to drive the pitch home and get the audience to act. If people have read this far into the copy, they want a result. Plain and simple. But they still haven't decided whether they are willing to pay the price. My job in this part of the process is to get them to decide on making an investment. To do so, I use the same subhead: "It's decision time." Then, I present the two choices and their consequences. The copy often reads something like this:

> There are two roads in front of you. You're at a crossroads. The road on the left leads to this. It's the same road you've always taken. It leads to the same results you've always received. The road on the right is a different road. It may or may not be more difficult. But the rewards are much greater and more in line with what you have been seeking as we've been spending this time together. I'm going to urge you to choose the right road.

This, of course, is a bit cheesy, but who cares? It works. Clever doesn't close. Clarity does. The point here is clear: When it comes to making a change, we have a decision to make. There's no sitting on the fence; we have to act. No matter what we do, including choosing to do nothing, there are going to be consequences on the other side of this decision. Understanding what those likely are helps us make better decisions now and forces our hand to do something sooner rather than later. Same goes for changing your life. You reach a point where you're done reading the books and listening to the podcasts and considering the proof. You know enough to act, and now it's time to go.

One of the most powerfully persuasive communication techniques is best summed up in a single word: "because." In *Influence*, Robert Cialdini cites a research study showing that simply adding the word "because" to a request multiplied the likelihood of compliance. Interestingly, the study seems to indicate that the legitimacy of the reasons supplied were not as important to the outcome as you might suppose. In fact, it seemed hardly necessary to have a real reason at all. For example, if you ask to cut in line at the post office, you will be more likely to get a "yes" response from the person in front of you if you say something such as "Would it be possible for me to please cut in front of you in line, because I'm really in a hurry?" That's hardly persuasive salesmanship, but having some reason is better than having none.

You should provide yourself with good reasons to buy whatever it is you're selling. As a practical matter, this means telling the truth. After my Parkinson's diagnosis, if I continued living the way I was before being diagnosed, I was going to die. I wasn't going to die right away, but my body was going to deteriorate at a faster rate if I kept drinking and waited for a miracle. So, I told myself, "I need to change the way I approach this, because my quality of life is already beginning to decline."

If you own a retail store and you want to sell your overstock of kitchenware, it's much better to just come right out and say, "We thought these would sell better. They didn't, and now we need to get rid of them. So, we put them on sale to motivate you to buy them." While that may not seem like brilliant copy—and it isn't—it does offer a legitimate reason for lowering the price of your merchandise. People respond to reason, and the result is usually profit for the seller.

People also respond to honesty and directness. This is not a new concept. John E. Kennedy, the "man who defined advertising," wrote an entire book on the subject called *Reason-Why Advertising*, which was published in 1904 and is now in the public domain. Kennedy is famous for calling advertising "salesmanship on paper" and argues in that book (which is more like a pamphlet) that to be an effective salesperson, you need to offer a reason for why you do everything. A good reason is the basis for everything we do, and without it, no matter how convincing our message may be, it will ring hollow and untrue.

People, before they can be persuaded, are primarily interested in themselves. To assume or expect otherwise is to invite failure. I like to use the phrase "What's in it for me?" or "WIIFM." When people go to a sales page, they don't want to know that a company was founded by the owner's great-great-grandfather, who got his start selling turnips out of the back of his truck on Highway 90. No, they want to know what this product can do for them. Perhaps these are magic turnips: turnips that can help you have better sex, or at least *have* sex. Likewise, to close the deal with yourself, you have to know what's in it for you. You have to ruthlessly appeal to your own self-interests and not give yourself any more credit than you deserve. On a sales page, I drive home the answer to WIIFM in the closing copy. This is where it all comes together, where you "set the hook," so to speak, with your prospect.

And in our case, that person is you. Remember that sales letter we wrote to ourselves? It's time to take it back out and write the final piece: the close. When it comes to creating change in your life, answering the "because" or "why" question is just like closing copy.

To do this well, first you have to recap the offer. Retell the story of what you're selling. Remind the reader (i.e., you) of the costs of not acting. Drive home the benefits. Reconnect to the outcome that had you interested at the start. Remind yourself of the guarantee and specifically what happens next. When it comes to getting a response from a potential buyer, your job as a copywriter is to elicit a decision. "Yes" is a valid answer, as is "no." The only response that's unacceptable is "I don't know" or silence. That is death to persuasion. You don't want to be in decision purgatory, the land of "maybe," which is the worst place for anyone to be. And since we're talking about changing your life, this is especially caustic. You can't live in no-man's-land when it comes to getting yourself out of whatever bind you've fallen into. You have to say yes or no.

Finally, the most important part of closing copy is asking for the sale. This is the biggest failure in face-to-face sales. People will spend hours prospecting, setting an appointment to make a presentation, preparing, and presenting, then not even ask for the sale in the face-to-face encounter. Why? The number one reason is the salesperson was afraid of rejection. But often, you only get one shot at a yes, and you've got at least a 50–50 chance. Why not go for it? There are always more prospects; the real battle is summoning the courage in the first place. Don't fail to ask for the sale.

In our case, this means asking yourself, "Do I buy into this? Am I willing to commit to whatever is required of me to get what I want?"

Say yes or say no, but do not delay in answering the question. It's time. Decide, then act.

The Five Templates

Your closing copy doesn't have to be long or complicated, but it does need to be effective. The best way to ensure this is a technique we are all familiar with in the direct-response world: swipe copy. Swipe copy is using someone else's sales letter template, then adapting it to your own needs and product. This is what many world-famous copywriters do, myself included. And it works just as well with personal transformation. Whenever we see someone lose weight or quit their job or do something extraordinary, we often ask what they did and how. The reasoning is pretty simple: if we know what they did to get what they have, we can do the same and have similar results.

There are five templates I use most often when writing closing copy, and they work well for me. You can easily adapt these templates to your own needs and apply them to your own journey of transformation. But first, let's talk about transitional copy. Transitional copy moves the reader out of the main sales copy and into the close. This transition comes after the guarantee, the bonuses, the pricing, and so on, and rolls into the final closing paragraphs or sentences of your sales letter. Here's the copy I used on myself:

"But What Can I Do? It's Too Late Now!"

Oh, please. Stop being a drama queen. You know that if you live, you still have a chance to clean up the mess you've made. But maybe just *one chance*. You're at the place, Sonny Jim, where you get no more do-overs.

You know you can get your life in order. And you also know that until now, you simply haven't wanted it badly enough to just go and *do the hard work.*

Here's the truth: The success you seek is simple, but not easy. You already know what to do. Here's the only question: *Will you actually do it?*

You can see that I've reconnected to the benefits. I've restated the big idea. I've reminded myself of the guarantee—and now I am moving to the close.

The "You Will Certainly Arrive" Close

This speaks to the inevitability of whatever actions your prospects are currently taking. It forces them to think about the future and what life will look like if they don't make a decision. An example of this would be: "Here's what you and I both know: one year from today, you will certainly arrive. The question is 'Where?' That is your decision to make right now." After that, you end the letter. Leaving the question open-ended invites the reader to answer it for themselves in a hopefully powerful and emotional way.

The Crossroads Close

This is the closing copy I referenced in this chapter. Using this template, you would follow your transition copy with something like the following: "You're standing at the crossroads. To the left is the same rough, rocky road you've been traveling. To the right is the road fewer people will choose. This road is not harder. It's different. Choosing the right road makes all the difference. I'm hoping you'll choose the right road today." This template is powerful because it plays on famous language that's deeply embedded in our subconscious from the Robert Frost poem "The Road Not Taken." I don't actually quote the poem, but I use language that is evocative of it. I also make the right road the correct one to choose. Choosing the right road makes all the difference. Choose the right option today. While that's not very subtle, it indicates the direction you want to go.

The Different Results Close

Are you a "quick and to the point" person? This closing copy is for you: "Here's the tough truth you probably already know. If you want different results, you need to do something different. Make a definitive decision right now to get different results." Cut right to the chase and talk about why this matters. If people want different results, they intuitively know they're going to have to do something different. This simply reinforces that existing belief and calls them to action.

The Decision Time Close

This closing copy is even more straightforward. Again, we have the transitional copy, and then we simply say, "It's been said that in your moments of decision, your destiny is shaped. What will you decide to do right now? The same thing you've been doing so you get the same old results? Or will you decide to change your results for the better by changing your belief?" Nothing super fancy or complicated about that. Nobody likes beating around the bush forever, and this close addresses the impatience we all feel with situations that we wish were different.

The Hand-Holding Close

Okay, this one might sound a little creepy when applied to yourself, but I think it still works. People don't like doing big, scary things by themselves, so we use this kind of close to remove the risk of having to do it all alone. It often reads like this: "And you won't be alone. I'm going to hold your hand every step of the way and walk you through this process." Since we're writing letters to ourselves here, you might want to speak to whatever deep fears you know that you have and assure yourself that you'll be okay. You might even spell out the details of how you will calm yourself down in times of stress, maybe through daily meditation, prayer, or self-care.

Give Yourself a Guarantee

All good sales letters should end with a guarantee. It helps you feel safe—secure. Let's start with this: a sad little guarantee, a weakling; one who's always picked on at the playground, always gets sand kicked in his face, and never makes a sale because he's not much of a guarantee. If I were writing myself a sales letter before I decided to change my beliefs, my guarantee would have looked something like this: "You can keep praying and visiting rallies, and if that doesn't work, then you get to try something else." You might say to yourself or to me, "That's not so bad." You know, you're right; it's not so bad! It's at least average, maybe even better than average, but it's not going to inspire the kind of confidence you need to take on the risk of changing your life. It is a sad little guarantee.

Let's go to work on this using the same example but changing the guarantee so it has some backbone. I'm going to role-play this for you, with me taking on the role of the salesperson and you being the client (but, to be clear, they're both actually myself).

"Ray," the client might say, "whatever I have to do to make my guarantee work so that you change the outcome of your life, I'll do it. I'll back up the guarantee I create, because I believe in you. I believe in you so much I'm willing to bet on it."

"All right," I would respond, excitedly, "let's do this thing."

First, I would start with a 100 percent take-your-decision-back guarantee. This means that if you are not pleased with the results of this new belief, you can take it back, plain and simple. I would offer this to myself as a way of putting my mind at ease and getting me to buy into the process. People are more likely to commit to things when they feel the risk is low or even nonexistent. The greater the risk, the greater the hesitation.

Next step is to integrate your USP, or unique selling proposition. In my case, I am a world-class marketer (or so my LinkedIn profile says), so my proposition was, "If I can sell a lawn mower to a herd of goats, I can make myself believe anything!" (No, I never did sell a John Deere to a pack of goats. But wouldn't that be something?)

After that, you want to personalize the guarantee. Yes, I know it's already personal because you're talking to yourself, but bear with me. Say something to yourself that you really mean, such as "I love you and want what's best for you. I want you to live a big, beautiful life. And if you walk with me, I'm going to lead you to it." That's personalizing the guarantee.

Next, give the longest possible guarantee. I gave myself a lifetime guarantee on my process. If at any point I didn't like my system for changing beliefs, I could, well, change it. This guarantee gave me faith in myself and took away the fear of commitment that comes with the top-five major life decisions (marriage, kids, divorce, changing beliefs, and whether pineapple goes on pizza—in that order). In the long run, I think you'll ultimately give yourself more chances at changing your life by offering the longest guarantee possible.

Then, make sure you emphasize that there are no strings attached. You can do so using very fancy, sophisticated language. Or you can just say there are absolutely no strings attached. You can change your mind at any time. A commitment like that becomes easy, because there's nothing permanent about it! If you can deliver what you promise, and you're willing to back it up this way, your guarantee will be almost irresistible.

The final step is to name the guarantee. That means spelling out exactly what you mean by "no strings attached." For myself, I spelled it out this way: "If you don't like this, if your life isn't improving, your spirit is in decay, and you find that the old way was better, then you can keep doing that. Old Ray can come back any time."

And that, my friends, is a guarantee.

When Life Calls You to Action

You may be at a time in your life when you don't need to convince yourself to take action. Something terrible has happened to you or a family member, and you know the only way out is through. It is quite literally a matter of taking action or dying. If you're in the middle of such a season, first of all, you have my deepest sympathy. It is one thing to choose to change your path, and quite another to expect to encounter a fork in the road and instead end up clinging for your life from the edge of a cliff.

I experienced this myself in 2020. My wife, Lynn, had a heart attack and nearly died. I wasn't completely self-absorbed at this point, but my life shifted from the mindset of "Help yourself stay well, Ray" to "Take care of Lynn at all costs." That was my call to action. It was a call to climb out of my own self-pity hole, get my head out of my rectum, and focus on my wife and what was important to her. So I took care of her. I took care of the house and took care of the dogs. I did everything I could to remove any stress from her life and made her the priority. It made our relationship one hundred times better. I don't recommend waiting for a heart attack to improve your relationship, but that call to action woke me up. It vastly improved our marriage experience. Her heart attack really underlined for me the question "What would it be like if she were gone?" Losing her would remove most of the meaning from my life. I've been with this woman for forty years now. The thought of losing her was my call to action.

If this situation applies to you, take another look at your sales letter. Ask yourself again: What is your motivation? Is it to help a loved one through a hard season? To be there for a close friend? Write another letter, this time with that person in mind. Once you know how to persuade yourself, you'll see all kinds of opportunities to make the lives of others better.

DO THIS

This book will do you little good if all you do is read it and nod safely, saying to yourself, "Yes, that is a good idea." If I convince you of anything, I hope it's that you actually have to write yourself a letter like the one I wrote. That's why I'm giving you these components. Take the time to go back through this chapter and write up the different sections, even borrowing the "templates" I've given you and adapting them to your own situation. Careful, though. You might find yourself changing in surprisingly powerful ways.

Chapter 12

Practice Becoming a New Person

 Most people are about as happy as they make up their minds to be.

—ABRAHAM LINCOLN

T HE BRITISH STATISTICIAN GEORGE E. P. BOX once said, "All models are wrong, but some are useful." A belief is a model for reality; it is not reality itself. Therefore, a model is not entirely accurate; in that sense, it is "wrong." But it can still be useful. When I started walking away from all the healing conferences and positive-thinking aisles of the bookstore, I began reading more scientific literature on Parkinson's. Whenever I adopt a new way of doing things, I always tell myself that this problem is temporary and I can always go back if I want. It's a mind trick to get myself fully involved. You can do what Bruce Lee did with martial arts: try a little of everything, keep what turns out to be useful, and throw out the rest. He is famous for borrowing many different ideas from different art forms, trying out all kinds of fighting systems and disciplines. And what he kept became part of his system. Many other martial artists disapproved of this approach, believing that pure adherence to a certain system, such as tae kwon do or kung fu, was better. But Lee's approach also meant that other martial artists could never figure out his methods, because he changed them all the time.

You can do the same with your beliefs, trying on new systems and borrowing different ways of being from various influences. Remember that your beliefs guide your actions and therefore your results. Trying new things to see what works is a wonderful way to get different, sometimes better results. Whatever helps you get closer to where you want to be—whatever makes you happier, healthier, stronger, wiser, richer—those beliefs are worth keeping.

After I realized my beliefs about my disease were destroying my life, I wanted new ways of being, so I began taking a few for a spin. For starters, I lived as though I truly believed Parkinson's could make me a better person. It was a simple belief but one that needed to take root. I began believing having this disease could make my business better and that working out and eating healthy would help me. I didn't know whether these things were true or even whether they would prove helpful, but I wanted to see how believing them could change my life. It was an experiment. The beliefs I have now are the ones that turned out to make my life better—the ones that worked (more on that later).

Change happens in partnership with a plan that represents a better vision for your life. Once you've researched all the possible ways to achieve transformation, from different marketing strategies to diet plans and financial advice, you have to pick the best path for you and commit to it. You're taking someone else's belief and trying it on now, experimenting with it to see whether it works. Committing fully to the process now is essential, even if only for a finite time, so that you can begin to see the results you want.

Alter the Environment

If we are going to "try on" a belief system, it has to be a system—which means it has to be defined. It has to be able to be written down. And then we have to figure out how to try it on. The way we do so is through our bodies, our internal thought patterns, and the environment. If you think about it, how else would information and beliefs come into our lives and be either reinforced or challenged if not through our five bodily senses, our internal thought patterns, and our environment? That's all there is for us, really. The body and the environment are so crucial. People think they are just going to change the way they think whenever they want to, but that doesn't work. That hasn't worked for anyone I know. You have to do other things to make that change in the way you think. New beliefs require a new structure around them.

When you go to one of these large-group awareness training events I mentioned, whether it's a revival service or a personal improvement seminar, one way the trainers change your belief system and indoctrinate you into their system is by changing your external circumstances. They have you wake up at a time you're not accustomed to and change your hydration schedule and even your eating schedule. These changes are intended to give you new thought patterns. All these external circumstances affect the body, so it stands to reason: mess with the body, change the beliefs. Changing the external environment, which includes your body and its surroundings, can change what happens internally.

So, when I want to change a behavior, I ask myself, "What are the triggers that lead to detrimental behavior?" They might include what I'm watching on television, looking at on the internet, or reading about. They may be the people I'm hanging out with, environments I'm putting myself in, or the amount of sleep I'm getting (or not getting). When I ask this question, I am looking for the factors that push me toward ways of thinking and being that I do not want to continue. Then I consider: "How can I change my thoughts, my body, or my environment so they are pushing me in the opposite direction?" Answering this question takes a lot of self-awareness—which is the reason most people never change.

Years ago, I was attending a conference, and Hale Dwoskin, whom I mentioned in chapter 7, was speaking. When Hale took the stage, one of the first things he said was, "Look, I don't want you to believe a word I say. Please test everything I tell you and see if it works for you. If it does, then great. If it doesn't, then ignore me." I thought that was enormously freeing then, but at the same time, it was kind of a honey trap to lure us in because we felt that we could trust him. He's the first person I ever heard say at one of these events, "I realize you may be skeptical. That's okay. I encourage you to let go of your skepticism just for the rest of today. You can have it back when you leave, if you want it."

Soon enough, I was paying $2,400 to fly to Sedona and spend two days with him. I don't begrudge him that. He was leading me to think new thoughts, which led to me paying him large amounts of money. Environments affect our thoughts, and thoughts change behavior. The way he framed his talk is a technique I still use to this day. When I think about changing my belief system, I think, *It's okay, I can have my skepticism back about this belief system if I want, but I'm going to try it out first.*

Expect People to React

Back when I was pursuing the miracle religious healing route, my wife and I decided to drive all around the United States in 2011 visiting revival churches that were part of a big healing movement. We visited Bethel Church, the International Church of Las Vegas, the International House of Prayer in Kansas, the Toronto Airport Christian Fellowship, and even a church that was built by Jim and Tammy Faye Bakker and came complete with a now-defunct Christian theme park. I was getting prayer from all these well-known healers. I made a decision at the time, which I did not share with my wife: I was going all in for a miraculous healing. I was going to do everything I could to have all these people pray for me. By the time we made our way through the whole circuit of religious revivals and got back to Washington State, I was going to be healed. And if I wasn't, then God and I were going to have to have a talk.

We got back, and I wasn't healed. At that point, I didn't feel like having a talk with anyone. If you change your beliefs, you end up eliminating people from your life. You have to decide what's negotiable and what's nonnegotiable. There was a point when my wife came to me and said that she was concerned about where I was going, because it felt as if I might be leaving her behind. I told her that it might feel that way, but that wasn't my intention. I said, "This doesn't change the way I feel about you. But right now, this isn't about you. This is about me. I've got to figure out where I am, where I'm going, and how I'm going to deal with all this. And I promise you that if we can keep talking, I don't have any intention of leaving you."

I would counsel others who are making changes in their lives to think about the possibility of this kind of reaction from people close to you beforehand. Changing what had been bedrock, nonnegotiable beliefs in your life may threaten the people who are closest to you. Some relationships may be nonnegotiable, and others not. If some people decide they don't want to be around you anymore, this may not actually strike you as a problem. But if there are people you care deeply for, then you've got to give some thought to the impact of your actions. It's not that you'd let their reactions stop you from seeking what's best for you, but you've got to at least consider the consequences. Decide what you're willing to do and what you're not willing to do.

The key for my wife and me was that we both agreed to not stop talking. We agreed to be honest with each other, and as a result, we are closer than ever, even closer than we were before the diagnosis.

That said, I did lose a lot of friends as I changed my life. As my friend Mike Kim says, "Sometimes people in your life may not make it through the upgrade." My upgrades meant leaning into a life I could love, even if my disease didn't go away. Changing my life meant I had to find a way to expand, and that meant trying new things. To change our environment, we have to change our behavior (and then that environment, in turn, influences what we do).

Move Toward What Feels Expansive

As my beliefs shifted, I began to question why I had been told certain activities were forbidden—whether that was doctors telling me not to travel or go to nightclubs, or pastors saying I shouldn't swear, dance, or get a tattoo. So I began to experiment with things that were "bad" for me, trying them in small doses to see what worked and what didn't. Drinking doesn't help my Parkinson's, so for the most part, I stay away from alcohol, but I do enjoy the occasional glass of bourbon. One time, I told a friend I wasn't going to drink anymore because it wasn't helping me, and he said, "Well, when did it help you?" I know what's going to happen when I do have some whiskey: My symptoms will ramp up. I won't sleep well. It doesn't help me. So I mostly stopped having it. And what I learned was that I can trust myself. I may make some mistakes, which are merely opportunities to learn. But I don't need some rule in my life about what's good or bad to tell me what I can clearly observe.

When I started getting tattoos, I got so many messages, emails, and phone calls from people quoting Bible verses at me, telling me I'd given my soul to Satan. My owl tattoo was especially heinous to people. They said owls are creatures of the devil. That was fun.

I also began doing things to challenge myself more, things I was afraid to do. One time I was hiking in Phoenix with my son, Sean. We got halfway through the hike, and I felt as though I wasn't going to be able to make it. Sean said, "Stop looking at the top of the mountain. Just look at the next turn of the trail." So I did that, and we got another quarter of the way up. But at that point I was on my hands and knees. I physically did not have the strength to stand up. I crawled the rest of the way, because I knew we were so close. I didn't want to quit. I crawled my way to the top. We stayed there for a long time, resting, looking at the view, talking to people as others came and went. Eventually, we started making our way back down, which was even scarier. I told myself that if I fell, I would need to just keep rolling. The whole experience was instructive to me; I learned I was capable of more than I thought—much more. The hike didn't kill me, after all. In fact, it helped me expand my thoughts about what was possible.

One of the dangers people run into, especially with anything traumatic such as chronic illness, is that their experience of the trauma forces them to act out of fear, shrinking the boundaries of their world. They get scared and get small. That can be a quick process of going down the drain, letting your life erode into death. If you stop traveling, stop hiking, stop walking, stop socializing, stop going out, it changes you. You become depressed and anxious. You start to wonder what the point of it all is. At least, I did for a while, and that was no life at all. So I became determined to not let my world shrink any more than it needed to. In fact, I wanted to expand it. On that hike, I expanded the horizons of what my body was capable of, and I learned about myself. By changing my body, I was changing my thought patterns. And it was all teaching me something.

On Practicing Becoming a New Person

No longer concerned with finding the be-all and end-all universal truth, I instead wanted to take action in ways that would allow me to live a better life, even with Parkinson's. I knew this step would begin with convincing myself that my diagnosis was a good thing, something I could use for the benefit of myself and others. And I knew an abundance of evidence would help me get there. So I started searching for reasons to believe that Parkinson's was, in some way, beneficial to me.

One of the ways I did so was by going back to that self-help section with my new "helpful belief" worldview and rereading every book I could get my hands on. No longer was I looking for "the answer." Rather, I was curious about trying different approaches to my problem and seeing what worked. Filling my mind with helpful, constructive words and ideas kept me going. Doing so continued to remind me what I was after and helped me see my disease as a gift, when before I had thought, *Are you kidding me? This is no kind of gift. Would you like me to give it to you?*

As a result of my changed response to the disease, I developed a lot more compassion for people. I developed more humility in my beliefs, as well. Today, I am more present with people, less con-cerned about the future, and more patient. It's become increasingly apparent to me that this is all I get, so I soak it up.

DO THIS

This is an invitation to try on a new belief. The belief is that life is happening for you, not happening to you. In other words, there is a reason for everything that has happened, and that reason is to do you good. You may not yet be able to see how that is even possible. That's okay. This is how we get stuck in thinking our situation is bad and there's nothing good about it. Just consider this idea for a moment, though. What if there was something good about your current situation, whatever it might be? Even if it seems ridiculous, write down something good that could come from this. Aim for ten ways this terrible situation in which you now find yourself is going to be good for you. Then watch what happens.

PART VI

Response—Making It Stick

What does it take to persuade yourself to live a better life? What does it take for you to believe something other than what you thought you knew for a very long time? Hint: It's not the truth. It's not being right or even having an accurate belief that changes a life. What it takes to change is motivation; and this is not an easy thing to understand, because everyone is motivated by something different. If you offer money as an incentive to someone who is driven by the need to feel significant, it won't work. Every human being operates on a slightly different currency, and that includes you.

This is the reason so much self-help literature doesn't actually work. Often, what you find in that space is some guru telling you what motivates them; you may borrow their motivation for a while, but if it ultimately doesn't resonate with you, it won't work. For example, some people think you need to live a life that matters or has "meaning," whereas others are completely content to simply enjoy their life without it needing to further some great purpose or cause. You can judge these tendencies as purposeless or narcissistic, but I think the simplest explanation is that everyone is motivated by something different.

This process is not about positive thinking. It's about positive action. Many self-help gurus teach that if you repeat a certain phrase enough times, you can hypnotize yourself into believing it's true. That rarely works, because most of the time, people don't actually believe it will. The way to change your life is to sell yourself on your own story first, to break down the process of what you want, how much it hurts to not have it, and what you want to happen. The cult of positivity has long taught us that if we recite a belief enough times with enough confidence, then it must come true. But how often does that happen? Positive thinking is never enough to pay the bills, make a dream come true, or help you live the life you want. What we need more than a series of chants and mantras is the power of persuasion. How you get what you want in life, business, or even relationships ultimately comes down to your ability to persuade. To achieve anything you want, you have to first convince yourself it's possible.

Chapter 13

Imagine the Worst

 Change happens when the pain of staying the same is greater than the pain of change.
—TONY ROBBINS

To help you make the right choices, you need to understand what is at stake. You can give yourself certain positive and negative consequences, as well. For example, I have a certain financial goal I want to hit in my life. When I reach that point, I am going to reward myself with the exact Tesla I want. Not only is it cool, but because it's self-driving, it will allow me to keep getting around as my symptoms increase and it gets harder to operate a vehicle on my own. When I wanted to lose sixty-five pounds, I made a public commitment on a website that said if I failed, I would contribute a lot of money to the political party I didn't like. I was going to have to make the donation public, as well. I lost sixty-five pounds.

Should we announce our goals to the world? There's a lot of

debate on this subject. Some people say you should keep your goals to yourself, but I think that's just setting yourself up for failure. Keeping goals private is an excuse to renegotiate the goal later and say to yourself, "Well, I really didn't want to do it anyway." It's the parable of the sour grapes: you say you want a thing, but when you can't get it, you tell yourself, "Well, it probably wasn't that good to begin with." Keeping a goal private often means you're not really committed to it.

If I Don't Change, How Bad Will It Get?

There is danger in ignoring real pain, real trauma, real problems. It's important and useful to acknowledge feelings and not bury them. It's also important to process them and decide what to do with them. It's very dangerous to continue wallowing in painful feelings. Wallowing won't help. So instead think: *This is bad now. If I don't change, how much worse will it be?*

I recognize that people can get in real deep trouble and become suicidal. My nephew was eighteen when he committed suicide. And we all wondered, "What happened?" We don't know what happened, because he seemed happy. There was some deep trauma that he had not dealt with at some level. Something was wrong—obviously. But then I think each of us, when faced with problems of any shape or size, almost always has an invitation at some point to answer this question: "How can I use this to serve me?" Even the person most married to their trauma will acknowledge that the reason they need to deal with their problem is so that it can serve them in some way and they can move forward with their lives.

Nobody wants to stay in the darkness, I don't think. The valid question is "How can I reshape the way I'm thinking about this so that it serves me?" Life is hard. During that year of growth and hardship, one of my best friends started buying into an apocalyptic view of what was happening. This pushed us and our families apart. These were good friends. We vacationed together. But suddenly I found us at odds every time we spoke. Now they're just gone. They were so convinced the apocalypse was here that there was no room for discussion. That was hard and still hurts. I think, *How did I miss that? What could I have said differently that would have helped them not be in the situation they are in now?*

In 2020, I had to lay off people from my business, and that hurt. I don't have the energy I once had to put in long days. In the past, I could always count on myself to show up and do what other people would not do. I can't count on that now. We had to make changes and adjustments to account for this, which led to all kinds of complicating factors. During the pandemic, I was unable to see either of my fathers (my biological dad and my stepdad). They both have serious health problems, and it was hard to not be in person with them for almost two entire years.

All I'm saying is that there are tons of things to feel bad about. They really do hurt, and I acknowledge that. In doing the reframing exercise, however, I realized there are tons of good things happening, too. Admitting the good does not discount the bad. I'm not denying bad things happened, but I am denying that those things can have first place in my thoughts. And I believe a "bad" thing can have positive outcomes, if we zoom out far enough or pay close enough attention.

We have a choice. I learned this a long time ago as a copywriter: when the way you're telling the story doesn't get the result you want, change how you tell the story. Find some way, some previously hidden perspective that allows you to turn a tragedy into a triumph, that helps you see the good in the bad—not in a reality-denying, dissociative way, but rather in a way that feels true to you. It is only then that transformation becomes possible.

Optimism Versus Pessimism

There was a long period when I, as an overweight and out-of-shape man, thought my health was mainly based on my genes. I had relatives who lived into their nineties or even to over one hundred who ate all the wrong stuff. My great-grandmother smoked a pipe, chewed tobacco, and ate starchy, fatty foods, including lots of bread, pancakes and syrup, donuts, and Ho Hos. You name it—if it's bad for you, she ate it. If it came in a box, she probably ate it. She lived to be almost one hundred years old with very few health problems. This led me to think I was special; it made me optimistic in the worst way.

There was a bumper sticker that read, "Eat right, exercise, die anyway." I thought, *Why make yourself miserable in the meantime?* But then when I got Parkinson's, I started doing the research, and I realized there were things I could do with diet and exercise that could mitigate symptoms, perhaps even slow the progression of the disease. Had I adopted a better diet and exercise earlier in my life, I might have developed the disease later; I might not have gotten it at age forty-five. Maybe, maybe not. I have no way of knowing, but the thought does haunt me.

When I decided to lose weight, it was because I realized that my excess fat was like the top of an iceberg. It was indicative of deeper issues. I had already run the ship into the iceberg, and now I was sinking. In order to get rid of the fat, I had to also get rid of excess fat in my thinking, increase my focus, and change my attitude. My thinking up until that point had been this: *I'm already married, I have a son, I have some money. Who really cares what I look like?* But there was more to losing weight than what I looked like. I went into hypercommitment mode and exercised every day. I ate a low-carb diet and stuck to it rigorously. I lost sixty-five pounds.

Plenty of people who are quite athletic, eat well, and are very, very healthy still get Parkinson's in their twenties or thirties. There's no guarantee I could have stopped the disease. But I've seen evidence that diet and exercise do make a difference. The best science we have today tells us that through epigenetics, we have a certain amount of control over which genes get expressed and which do not, based on our diet, our environment, our exercise routines, and even our thoughts. How we use our body, the foods we eat, the environment we place ourselves in, and even the way we think about things all apparently have a very strong impact on the expression of certain genes.

Lots of repeatable experiments show that if we stay physically active, eat in a way that doesn't cause our bodies to deteriorate (avoiding lots of sugar, for instance), and practice mindfulness, we can watch as certain genes are turned on or turned off. These outcomes are repeated from subject to subject. This effect seems to be true, as far as we can tell, in the context of the information we have now.

This research tells us that our genetic destiny is not predetermined. We may be predisposed to go in a certain direction, but we have lots of control over that. Why else would identical twins end up with totally different genetic destinies? One twin gets lung cancer, and the other one doesn't, but one smoked. I believe that living with the worldview that you might be wrong, and having the humility to accept new information, could actually make you healthier—as long as we form our beliefs from a place of informed, realistic optimism.

The Power of Consequences

The point here is not to initiate you into a doom-and-gloom methodology that assumes the worst is yet to come. The point is to help you tell yourself what *could* happen if you don't act. A lot of sociological studies have been done about optimists versus pessimists. The studies show that optimists tend to have a better quality of life. Qualitatively, they feel better about their lives; obviously they would. What's not obvious is that optimists actually have better outcomes in their lives. You can track that finding with empirically measurable criteria: optimists do better financially, physically, and in their relationships. And it is not because their worldview is more accurate. An optimist's actual view of the world, many people have determined, is not as accurate as that of a pessimist. But optimists' belief in a better outcome is so strong that they influence their external environment to get better outcomes, even though these weren't "realistic" initially. Optimists make a better outcome realistic through the way they think about it, which controls the way they feel about it, which controls the way they act, which alters their results.

We often need both positive and negative consequences, depending on what the potential outcomes are. And often, pain is a better motivator than pleasure. That said, there are people with extraordinary self-discipline who keep their goals to themselves and crush them, no problem. I am not one of those people. Knowing what I know about myself, I need both: the positive reward to draw me forward and the negative consequences to prod me in the behind. I think that's true for most people. The fear of negative consequences forces us to act now versus later, and the positive reward that comes with the action reinforces our desire to take action.

And then, there is the importance of community.

The Importance of Community

Surrounding yourself with a community that will encourage you in making the right choices for you is critical in changing your life. For me, this usually comes in the form of masterminds. These small groups of peers have been an integral part of my journey, and right now, I am a member of three such groups.

Like any other group, a mastermind group is only as useful as you allow it to be. In my experience, it's better to have a small, closely held circle that keeps you accountable to what you say you're going to do and with whom you can be totally transparent than it is to be part of a larger, less personal group. Of course, large communities can be useful, as well; they help us feel that we're a part of something bigger than ourselves, whether that's a church or a synagogue or a political party. There's nothing wrong with feeling that you belong to something important. But the downside is that the larger the group, the less the transparency. So you need to find a way to find small groups of peers who help you get where you want to go.

Of course, every group will have its own dogma and rules that may, in some way, constrain you. But they can also guide you. As Joe Rogan once said, "Every single religion that has ever been on the face of the Earth, ever, is a cult." You can substitute "self-help guru" for "religion," and the validity of the statement is the same. Too harsh? Perhaps. Then again, any group of humans is going to be flawed in some way, because no one can tell you who you are or what you should do. Other people can only help guide you, giving you clues about the right direction for you and keeping you accountable to whatever you decide.

One of the groups I belong to is a mastermind of five men I've met with once a week for years. I tell these guys everything: the good, the bad, the ugly, and then some. They do the same with me, as far as I can tell; and the result is all kinds of incredible transformation. We've walked one another through seasons of growth and loss, failure and success, and everything in between. I'm fine with being a part of a group for a specific purpose. If it's for business only, that's fine, but I also needed a group that is for more than business, which is what these five guys are for me. Transparency is key; I need to be able to tell them anything, including how I feel in the moment, even if I'm upset or thinking irrationally. They show up for me, accepting me as I am and reminding me of what's important to me.

I found this group by accident. I was good friends with and trusted a couple of guys I already knew; I knew they were both part of a mastermind group, and I was curious about being a part of something like that. It wasn't a paid group, just a group of peers, but it was closed, so the group wasn't accepting new members. I asked them if they knew of any other group like theirs that I could become a part of, and they responded that they were putting my name in for consideration to join the group. Within a few days, they got back to me and asked if I'd like to join. I told them I would, and they unanimously voted to accept me into the group. I became the sixth member of that five-member group, and that changed everything.

It's important to note that this happened because I asked. Communities often take work, and becoming a part of a group that will help you often takes initiative. It doesn't just happen. If you sit around and wait for a supportive community to come along and form around you, it almost certainly won't. Something will happen, but probably not what you're wanting. Don't be discouraged when there are some false starts, when you try to join a few groups that you think might get you but then just don't. It's normal for this to not work. You have to keep trying. Hell, you might go out into the desert to do mushrooms with somebody and find out that the guy is really freaking weird. Imagine that. Don't be afraid to walk away from people who aren't going to help guide you to where you want to go. Doing so isn't selfish; it's good for everyone.

A Final Wake-Up Call

One of the last trips I took before the 2020 pandemic locked everything down was to California, and it was a wake-up call. The person I was traveling with had to take another flight on the second leg of the journey, since lots of flights were already canceled due to the sudden panic. I ended up stuck at the Delta counter of the Oakland airport, unable to walk, in a wheelchair, by myself. Eventually someone wheeled me from the terminal to the curb, and I was bused to a hotel. I stayed the night by myself. It was a pretty striking moment: the uncertainty of the pandemic combined with feeling utterly helpless and alone. I had a big pity party.

That night, reality set in. I realized there would be no more travel, at least not for quite some time, and that all my speaking gigs would be canceled. All live events scheduled for the year were over. Most of my income at the time depended on the work done at these live events, so this worried me. People paid a premium to attend these events—anywhere from $3,000 to $10,000 per ticket—and attendees almost always left satisfied with the experience. The events had a high return on investment for the business, as well, since we would sell other products and services. Our whole team made sure it was a very high-end experience for the attendees: nice hotel, meals provided, and support staff attending to their every need. I did all the teaching, which became harder and harder as my health worsened but was something I still enjoyed. And now, it was all over. There were also events not hosted by my team but at which I was paid to speak, and those were gone, as well. Everything, it seemed, had fallen apart overnight.

Meanwhile, bills kept coming in, and money was short. I stopped opening the bills, too scared to face reality, and threw them straight in the trash. Things were starting to look bleak. On top of that, my health began to decline. I had surgery on my rotator cuff, which put me completely out of commission for several months. I felt as though I was barely conscious at the time. It was my right shoulder, which is also the side of my body that is most affected by Parkinson's. One of the key things about rotator cuff repair surgery is that after surgery, you must keep your shoulder as still as possible. I have Parkinson's disease, which means I shake a lot, and keeping my right shoulder still is impossible. The orthopedic surgeon shrugged and said, "Just do the best you can." It took me the better part of a year to recover.

That year, 2020, was crisis time galore, some of it of my own making, some of it due to the pandemic, and some due to my illness. Most shocking was Lynn's heart surgery. Once again, I began to question a lot about my life. Here I was, years into this experiment with rebuilding my beliefs, wondering how I could persuade myself to live a better life, and I had so much guilt and shame about how terrible my life had gotten. However, I realized these challenges didn't disqualify me from a better life; in fact, they qualified me for one—because, once again, things had finally gotten bad enough for me to do something.

DO THIS

Often, it's not just beliefs or ideas we need to change. The consequences of our beliefs may be in the form of a job, a house, a group of friends, even a religion. The list is obviously endless. As we make a change in the way we think about life and what we believe, it becomes necessary to leave some of those things behind. This can be frightening, but it can also be exciting. Make a list of what (or even who) you might need to leave behind to live the life you desire. Don't feel bad about this; it's only an exercise, and it's just between us for now.

Chapter 14

Remove All Risk

 So we shall let the reader answer this question for himself: Who is the happier man, he who has braved the storm of life and lived or he who has stayed securely on shore and merely existed?

—HUNTER S. THOMPSON

WHEN I FINALLY "WENT PUBLIC" with my Parkinson's diagnosis, one of my friends said quite plainly, "Well, you've got it, so how are you going to use it?" And that really pissed me off. *What an arrogant, presumptuous thing to say,* I thought. The more I thought about it, though, the more I realized he had asked me the most useful question anyone had asked since my diagnosis. What *was* I going to do with my diagnosis? Contemplating this question, I began to see how I could develop more empathy for people who suffered from diseases that were incurable, especially those that were degenerative and affected the very root of behavior, appearance, and ability. I also found a new identity in something deeper than whether I could button my shirt or use a fork. What was I going to do with my diagnosis? I was going to find all the ways it might serve me and improve the lives of everyone I cared about. And that was one hell of a challenge.

Slowly, through trial and error, I began to construct a new worldview, one that was more satisfying than "I'm sick, and it's all my fault." I began to appreciate that there are certain things in life we may not ever get to understand, and what we do with those mysteries is how we choose to live our lives. For so long, I thought life was happening to me, but soon I saw it was happening for me. I might not get to choose the exact circumstances of my life, but I did have some control over what I made of it. And that was enough. Taking my friend's advice, I made a decision to believe my Parkinson's diagnosis could, in fact, be good. Now, this disease is awful, and I would never wish it on anyone; it has made the most rudimentary aspects of my life incredibly difficult. But the Parkinson's has also made many other things possible. It's made me a better husband, father, and leader, forcing me to make changes I had wanted to make for quite some time but that I otherwise would have ignored for many more years.

What was it that created this positive change in my life? The disease itself? Of course not. What made my life better was belief. Not just any old belief, though—a better belief, one that worked. Since that decision, a lot has happened, and I'm still figuring out what it all means. I don't believe God gave me this disease. I don't believe it's karma paying me back for something bad I did. I don't believe I did anything to deserve this. At best, my situation seems the result of random chance or, at worst, an attack enacted by a malevolent force in the world. But the truth is I don't know and don't believe I can know. What is within my power is the ability to look at my situation and say, "How can I use this?" I can't always turn it into exactly what I want, but I do have the power to believe.

When you think about what's best for you, look at everything you're encountering in your life, and ask yourself, "Does this contribute to the identity I'm creating for myself? Or does it lead me back to where I was before?" Everything in life is information, and it is all confirming what is already true or what we want to be true. If what we have in front of us says, "You're still the same person you were before," then it's hard to break out of that identity. Sometimes we don't grow because we have too much stuff in our lives conflicting with what we're trying to construct. If you tell yourself, "I'm an organized person and have a minimalist aesthetic for my home," but your house is a chaotic mess, then that creates dissonance and will cause you to disconnect from what's real. It's hard to live into a new identity in an old place. Your current identity is too real and too much in your face to ignore. It's important to change the information you receive to reinforce the beliefs you want.

If part of your new identity is that you are a minimalist and only own things that are beautiful or useful, then get rid of everything other than that. Reinforce the belief through action. As Zig Ziglar once said, "You cannot climb the ladder of success dressed in the costume of failure." Response is how we create our new reality now, reinforcing the beliefs we want to believe with clear and decisive action.

If something isn't serving you, you can always let it go—as I did with my regular drinking. When you write a sales letter to sell a very expensive training program to someone, what's one of the fundamental elements you always include? The guarantee. *It's risk-free. If it doesn't work, you can get your money back. It's not permanent.* I look at changing beliefs the same way. I can go all in, dive in as deep as I can go. I'm going to play this game as if my life depends on it. If it doesn't work out, I can return it. If the new beliefs don't work, I can trade them back in for my old ones. I've found, though, that I rarely conduct an experiment like this one and then turn around and go right back to where I started. I usually end up with some modified version of beliefs, based on the new information I received in the process.

That said, I try to be realistic here. I do not make my decisions in a vacuum. I have friends, family, and employees who depend on me for their livelihood. I frequently have to decide, "Would I rather be ruthless, or would I rather be in this relationship?" Some things are just not important enough to ask someone else to change something about themselves to make me happy. It's more important that they're happy so that I can share in their happiness and we can be happy together. I don't view this as a compromise so much as reasoned decision-making. It's not an excuse, not a way to let myself off the hook; rather, it's a way to be conscious and honest about what I value most. Every decision has a consequence, and the right one might simply be the one we make when we consider all the options and outcomes. That's when we "get it."

As with the scientific method, you test the belief, and if the results are working for you, then you keep believing. If not, you modify the belief in some way and try again. In marketing, a guarantee that works is one that reduces the amount of risk the customer is taking to almost zero. They're not going to be worse off than when they began. The fact is, action and inaction both have consequences. You'll either keep getting more of what you've been getting, or you're going to stumble into something different. My suggestion is this: Instead of having those things happen accidentally and randomly, why not take conscious control of the process? What might take twenty years could be done in three months.

I had to persuade myself that my life wasn't just one degenerative journey into the abyss. One clear moment in my life when I started believing that it was possible to change my beliefs was on the seventh anniversary of my diagnosis. When I was first diagnosed, my neurologist painted a pretty grim picture of my prognosis. He said that in seven years, my life would look pretty bad—I wouldn't be able to work or get around, certainly not travel—and in many ways my life would be unmanageable. After that first consultation, I went home and did my research, discovering the practice I had just been to was the best in the entire Northwest. So I went back to the same practice again, but this time asked to see the other neurologist there, who painted the same horrible picture the first physician did. So I got depressed and considered taking my life a few times.

Seven years later, my life was nowhere near as bad as what they had described. In fact, in many ways it was much better. Although I had not eliminated the disease from my body, I was certainly doing a lot better than they thought I would. That was when I knew my belief was working, when I believed it was working.

A belief is working when it produces the quality of life you want to be experiencing—because why else would you have the belief, right? But all of us have unconscious beliefs, too: beliefs we didn't choose that may be helpful or harmful. If you believe that working out is going to make you feel better, look better, or live longer, and if that's not true, you're not going to keep working out. The belief doesn't work for you. This is my invitation to you: feel free to give up all of the unconscious beliefs that aren't working for you and adopt new ones that could work better. It's not wrong to get to the root of your beliefs. It's one of the best ways to love yourself better: by paying attention to what you believe and understanding why. Only then can you change your beliefs, and only then can you live a better life.

This, in the Christian world of healing and miracles, is what we might call "testing it"—the place where we see whether what we believe is actually true. In copywriting, it's what I call the response, the point where the reader takes action, typically resulting in buying something. For our little experiment in this book, the response means moving beyond the plan into a place of action. But before we do so, we have to understand who it is we want to be and realize we can practice becoming that person now.

A lot of positive-thinking approaches fall short at this point. They stay stuck in the "being" of things without immediately following it with action. But the truth is the being part is simply imagining who you want to become and trying to feel deeply from that place. I won't belabor this part of the process too much, because I see a lot of folks push this to an unhealthy point, as if all you have to do is believe hard enough. That, clearly, is not true. As someone once said to Jesus, "I believe! Help my unbelief." What we want to reconcile here is that you don't have to believe more or hustle harder. You can choose to live a certain way without any explanation or reason. You can simply choose to believe and act the way you want, because that's what you chose.

Four Questions to Consider When Deciding to Act

But how do you know what is the right choice for you? Do you just pick one randomly and hope for the best? Do you make a detailed list of pros and cons? What's the process for finding out what the next step is? In my experience, there are four criteria to examine why we're doing anything and whom it benefits. Asking yourself these questions can help you figure out whether something is the highest and best use of your energy, your time, and yourself:

1. Do I enjoy this?
2. Is it good for me?
3. Is it good for others?
4. Does it serve the greater good?

The highest level of activity or endeavor we can engage in is when the answer to all four of these questions is yes. Yes, it feels good. Yes, it's good for me. Yes, it's good for others in my life. And yes, it serves the greater good, at least insofar as I can tell. Anything less than this standard is less than the best we're capable of experiencing.

So let's look at the nuances of answering these questions, because the process is rarely so simple as getting four yeses and going for it. For example, exercise is good for you, but it doesn't always feel good. At least, it didn't for me at first and sometimes still doesn't. But if I stick with it long enough, I always feel better and am always glad I did. I've learned to anticipate that feeling. When I get ready to go exercise, I remind myself that I'm going to feel great because I'm doing this—not just because I'm proud of myself for exercising, but because I will actually have more energy. I will also have more neurological control over my body and my brain. Exercise causes neurochemical changes and the epigenetic effects that I'm after—slowing down, reversing, or even eliminating this disease from my life. Even if I can just ameliorate my symptoms a little bit, it's better than taking a pill. Exercise works. I enjoy it, it's good for me, it's good for others (because when I feel better, I can lead and influence others better), and this serves the greater good.

Even if something initially does not feel good, you can change your mind about that. Coffee is a common example for most people. The first time you drank it, did you think, *Man, that's delicious! I want some more of that!*? I doubt it. My first reaction was, *Good God, how can people drink this?! It's as though I heated up tar, diluted it with water, and boiled it over a medieval campfire.* But I learned to like coffee and even became addicted to it. I've done the same thing with exercise. All my life, I loathed it, but I paid a price for that, and I understand that now. So I've changed the experience of exercise from something I don't enjoy to something I do. If you know something is good for you, but you don't enjoy it, you can change that—either by finding a version of the activity that you do enjoy or by simply changing your beliefs about the activity.

That said, there's nothing wrong with enjoying what you do and pursuing what feels good. Plenty of people want you to believe you shouldn't do what you want, because doing so would be "selfish." But in my experience, every time I work on myself, I benefit others. Certain institutions want us to believe that if we want something just for ourselves, then we're being selfish. Why do they do that? Because they are worried we're going to do something they don't like. Maybe we'll give our resources to someone else. I hate to be blunt, but some churches would rather we give our money to them than grow our own financial wealth.

Doing what's best for you is often what's best for everyone else.

Shoulder the Risk

When it comes to sales, we need to remove fear, so that people are free to buy. Before we do that, we have to understand where this fear comes from. In any transaction, there is risk on both sides. However, there's a secret you need to know about your prospects. And since in this case, you are your prospect, it's a secret you need to know about yourself: You *want* to be right. You want to buy into this belief you're selling yourself. Why? Because you want your life to change. You want to be better. You want to feel better. You know there's something more to life than the one you're living.

The challenge is that you know you can't take a simple idea at face value. You need proof that this is a belief worth investing your life in. You must remove the barrier, the fear of doing what you want to do: to buy into embracing a new belief. How do you remove that barrier? Shoulder the risk. Simply by telling yourself, "It's okay if this doesn't work for me," you remain free to keep moving, to try other things.

Armed with this knowledge, you can sell to yourself with confidence. You have so much confidence in what you're offering that you are willing to bet on it. You're going to put your money on the line. You're going to put your money where your mouth is. How do you convey this message? First, you have to *get* the message. You have to really feel this way. Now I know you're thinking, *Ray, how can I believe something I don't yet believe because I'm convincing myself to believe it?* Well, I'll tell you how. You don't have to believe the new belief. You just have to believe it will be okay if it doesn't work out.

In the case of throwing away my old belief system for the Wild West of science and medicine, I knew I didn't have much to lose as far as my health was concerned. Sure, I tried out atheism for a while, but it wasn't ultimately satisfying. And guess what? God was right there where I left him. Only this time, when I started praying again, it wasn't a prayer for miracles.

What You Fear the Most

What do you fear the most? I bet it isn't being wrong or losing friends or feeling stupid. Those things are a hassle, to be sure. But we are willing to endure all kinds of nonsense for the sake of true and lasting transformation. What we don't want to go through is the trouble of breaking down old beliefs and investing in a new way of seeing the world only to discover that this way doesn't work any better. Well, I hate to tell you, but that's life. If you ever want to grow, to live better, to change, you're going to have to deal with a lot of trial and error. What most people fear, I think, is failure—that is, not getting what they want. But this is inevitable and somewhat necessary. Your job, then, is to remove that fear. Be confident in yourself and your ability to roll with the punches. You can do this. What's harder than change is staying the same. Let's exchange the fear of failure for the fear of stagnancy.

DO THIS

One of my favorite devices to help alleviate doubts and fears in the mind of the person I'm writing to is something I learned from one of my marketing pals, Russell Brunson. He calls these the "if onlies." As you think about the changes you're seeking to make in life, for each significant change write out a sentence like, "If the only thing making this change did for me was . . ." And then fill in the possible benefit. Maybe making a particular change in your diet will cause you to live longer. So your first "if only" might be, "If the only thing this diet did for me was add another three years to my life, it would be worth any discomfort or inconvenience I might experience." Write up as many "if onlies" as possible for each change you want to make. Then conclude that list by writing something like the following: "The change I am making doesn't do one single thing on this list. *It does them all.*"

Chapter 15

Commitment Has a Cost

 *I've learned that you shouldn't go through life with
a catcher's mitt on both hands; you need to be able
to throw something back.*

—MAYA ANGELOU

THE WAY YOU THINK IS what limits the very growth you
want. Sit with that for a moment. We are coming to the end
of our road here, and it's time to make the change you want to see
stick. So, let's put the past in the past. It's easy to get caught up
in the idea that things are a certain way, and that's just the way
they're going to be. But that simply isn't true. Remember what
Werner Erhard said: "The world does not care what you intend,
how committed you are, how you feel, or what you think." The
world, he argued, moves when you act. And that's where we are at
now: at the very point of action.

Wherever you are in life now, there is no judgment. Know that the past is in the past. Learn from it; celebrate it, or grieve it, if you must; then move on, because what is written is written, my friends. The future, however, is yours to create—if you commit to it.

But how?

First, don't make this only an intellectual exercise and say, "Okay, I'll put the past in the past." Get out your journal and write out your feelings about the situation you've been pondering as you've read this book. A good way to get your feeling juices flowing is by following the emotion wheel. If you don't know what that is, google it, and send me a thank-you card later. Think of this specific event and identify each emotion that is stirred up. Why do you feel that way? Write it down.

Once you've identified your emotions, examine the thoughts that you've written down on paper and ask yourself, "Is this really what I believe? Is this really what I want to be thinking going forward? Or do I need to clean this up and shift the way I think about this?" The answer will reveal itself to you. This journal exercise will help you tangibly connect with what's going on inside you.

Second, define your objective. What do you hope to accomplish by changing your beliefs? People tend to make this inquiry so complex, but it doesn't have to be. Just write down what personal wins you want to have accomplished in the next twelve months. Think carefully about your goals. Once you select them, set them in stone; your beliefs may change, but your objective doesn't.

And third, schedule your plan. Obviously you can't set your clock by your feelings and beliefs, but a plan inspires action, and action is what we want here; this isn't a passive assignment. You can't change your life by sitting in the backyard and watching the birds at the feeder, pleasant as that activity is.

Here's the rub: you have to create an irresistible offer—an offer so good, you can't refuse it; so good that you would have to be an absolute idiot not to accept the offer. You now understand the theory behind your beliefs, maybe why you believe them, and why you want to change. You know how to motivate yourself to action. So now what? This is your final pitch. If this were an email marketing campaign, it's the last message I'd send before I check out of the customer's inbox for good.

How do you create an irresistible offer? As Alex Hormozi explains in his book *$100M Offers*, one way to create an irresistible offer is to approach the problem not logically, but psychologically. Most people, he explains, try to solve problems with logical solutions, but this is what everyone else has done. If the solution to your problem were entirely logical, the problem would have been solved by now. Therefore, the only problems left to solve are the illogical ones, those created by people's emotions. That's what Hormozi means by a psychological problem and solution. Find the feeling in the problem, and you've discovered the key to solving it. Sounds familiar, right? The good news is, you've already set the foundation for creating an offer so good you can't refuse it. We've been looking at our situations like marketers, identifying the pain behind the problem. Now, you're going to offer a magic solution to yourself.

Are you ready? Buckle up.

The OPEN Scale

I teach something in my copywriting course called the OPEN Scale. This is the scale of buyer awareness that there's a problem in their life—a problem for which you have the solution, namely, a product you sell. The levels of awareness can be summarized by the acronym OPEN.

First, the O in OPEN stands for "oblivious." Potential customers don't know they have a problem and don't know whether there's a solution. So they don't care. Maybe this is where you were before you read this book. You could feel stuck in a mire, but you didn't know it and you really didn't care. Oblivious equals hard to sell to.

Then, for the *P*, there are the people who are "pondering"; they are thinking about your solution. This is a person who, for instance, feels a headache coming on. They've had headaches before, they feel a headache coming on, and they say to themselves, "You know, I might need to get some headache medication at some point."

The next level, *E*, is "engaged." Now the person's head is beginning to hurt—to pound. The person says to themselves, "I need to get some headache medicine. As soon as this meeting's over, I'm going to jet out to the drugstore and get some Tylenol."

After "engaged" is the *N* level: "need." Need says, "My head is splitting. I'm in so much agony. If I don't get some kind of medication, I'm going to have to pull the covers over my head and sleep for the next twenty-four hours. Or maybe I'll run my head through this wall." If you've ever had a migraine, you know what I'm talking about. A person with a migraine will pay whatever needs to be paid to get relief from that migraine or cluster headache. I've had both. I know what they feel like. You don't want them. You'd pay anything and you'd do almost anything to avoid getting those kinds of headaches, because they're debilitating. That's a person in need.

Which person would you rather sell to: someone who's oblivious, pondering, engaged, or in need? Obviously, the person who's in need. And, news flash, you're the person in need! So what's the closest you can come to giving yourself a magic solution to your need? That's the kind of irresistible offer you want to make to yourself—a magic solution to the need you have right now.

When you enter into that realm where you've got a dream solution, and you can give it to yourself fast, almost instantly, you can do so frictionlessly. You take all the reasons that would stop you from buying into your new belief out of the way. If you have a preponderance of proof, as we discussed earlier, you can add two more elements—your dream solution and urgency—and get there.

See how this is building?

The Dream Solution

What do you hope to accomplish? What's the change you want to create? In my situation, I had hoped to stop feeling butthurt that God wasn't healing me and to be able to take actions (with results) to improve my quality of life. That was my dream solution that was based in reality. We all need to start from a place of desire, of what we want that helps overcome the pain and discomfort standing in our way.

So think about what you want. Write it down. Go big or go home, friend, because we're almost to the finish line. That thing you wrote? *That's* your irresistible offer. That's the offer you can't refuse. You have the power to take action in your life and create the change you need. Because, guess what? You have to believe you can make the change in order for it to work. Just as I believed the right diet would help me reverse the effects of aging, you have to believe that following X will help you achieve Y. Now it's probably not possible to reach an instant transformation in your life when you're changing your beliefs, but by following the PASTOR method, you've eliminated most of the friction.

Whatever your objections to changing—fear, doubt, or discomfort—you have removed all the friction you possibly can from the process so that it is virtually frictionless. There is now no hindrance to getting what you want out of life, other than bad beliefs. You just have to give yourself a preponderance of proof, then connect it to a series of actions that get you where you want to be. Personally, I have stacks of articles I've researched on diets, lifestyle, and what I've tried myself that back up the approach I'm taking today. Do the same. Collect all the evidence you need—more than you think you need—to prove to yourself this belief you're pursuing is the best possible thing for your life.

Operation Mindset Magnet

There is one more element you need to add to your offer to make it truly irresistible: urgency. You have to act fast, because this offer is good for a limited time. This is where you answer the question "What happens if I don't do this?" I want you to really think about that. You've read through an entire book, pondering your life and how you can change it. So now ask yourself, "What happens if I don't?"

Now bear with me and my New Age juju, but you want to attract the solution and beliefs you seek. This is called magnetism. If you put that energy, that question, that need out into the world, it's going to bring you what you're asking for. You're trying to attract, or magnetize. This means you have to engage in the right activities to change your beliefs, so you can attract the right people and the right situations. You must ruthlessly eliminate all other actions and activities until you have accomplished what you set out to do.

Then, you put it all together. This is how you can make all this practical, something you can actually do today. First, commit to the challenge of changing. Then, give yourself an offer so good you can't refuse it. And finally, find a way to market the solution to yourself every single day. Yes, every day. If you believe in your solution, then you believe it works. And all beliefs need continued support and evidence to survive. But how do you continue to support your belief without boring yourself and becoming numb to what you're saying? Tell good stories. Get creative. You have to make a connection between the stories you're telling yourself and the offer you want to receive.

We've Always Believed in Stories

When I was a child, my parents read me stories—the Bible, Aesop's Fables, classic fairy tales and Disney's take on them. As a young boy, I daydreamed I was a character in the stories of Superman and Batman. I was Will Robinson befriending an alien robot and saving his family in the old series *Lost in Space*. I was part of *The Swiss Family Robinson*, riding ostriches and building a fortress high up in a tree. Storytelling, from the time we're children, is a way of understanding ourselves, making sense of the world, and dreaming up what we want out of life.

Dr. Milton Erickson was probably the most identifiable proponent of storytelling as a way of psychotherapy. Dr. Erickson changed people's psychology for the better by telling them stories or by engaging in stories they were already telling themselves and then helping alter the course of those stories. He was a master at working with stories this way, and he did so almost intuitively. Psychotherapy and even hypnosis come down to telling a story the person is willing to believe. Hypnosis involves a suspension of disbelief, a state in which you've relaxed the focus of your mind enough to entertain the imaginary ideas of stories as a different framework with which to view the world. But it's not just through hypnosis and psychotherapy that we use stories to alter people's perception of reality.

Movies, books, fairytales, and even our own imaginations are filled to the brim with stories we tell ourselves—stories we sometimes choose to believe.

Stories capture our imagination. We imagine ourselves in stories all the time as we think about how we're going to deal with certain situations in our lives. Thinking about the reason our spouse is late for dinner, for example, we can imagine that they are having an affair, they were in an accident and are hospitalized, or they got lost and popped a tire hitting a pothole too hard on the wrong side of town. Our whole lives, we're making up stories. And we begin to physiologically experience the reality of the story, whether it's true or not. Our blood pressure goes up, our heart begins to hammer, we can't think straight. We're consumed with jealousy or rage or love. Whatever that story we're telling ourselves generates internally is what we experience.

Look at the stories that were told during the recent pandemic. Conspiracy theorists had a variety of stories to tell. There wasn't just one conspiracy, but many. The vaccines were a mark of the devil. They implanted a chip that would go to your brain and that the government would then use to track you. Then there was a conspiracy that the conspirators were conspiring against the people who bought into the theories. The conspirators worked for the Illuminati, or they were in it for the money, or they just followed the hype. There were many conspiracy theories, on both the political right and left. And undoubtedly, each of them contained an element of truth. But that's the oldest trick in the book, isn't it? You can spin any story you want as long as it's based on a little bit of truth. Every lie contains some element of truth to make it more palatable, more believable. I even found myself swaying from one narrative to another because they were presented more compellingly at different times. But whatever story we bought into, whatever narrative we followed during the pandemic, that's the story we believed. That's the reality we chose to live in.

We function on stories. We learn from them. It's how we understand. If someone says to you something like "Oh, that's just sour grapes," they may not even know that saying originated from one of Aesop's Fables. Most people probably do know that "Slow and steady wins the race" is from the story about the tortoise and the hare, also one of Aesop's Fables. Both those stories are 2,500 years old or even older, and we are still using them to understand our world. So for us to be better persuaders, we need to master the art of telling great stories. And if we want to persuade ourselves, telling great stories to ourselves is really important, as well.

The Closing Question

This book has been about change, and change starts with what you believe. But at the core of every belief, and even at the core of this book, there is a story. Now, you're at a crossroads. You can put this book down, mark it on the list of books you've read for the year, and forget about the whole thing. Or you can do something daring—something brave. You can ask yourself, "What stories am I telling myself? What reality am I living in?" And even more important, "What stories am I willing to believe?"

CONCLUSION:

Read This . . . and LIVE!

 I have come to understand that life is best to be lived and not to be conceptualized. I am happy because I am growing daily and I am honestly not knowing where the limit lies.

—BRUCE LEE

I WAS AT HOME IN THE kitchen, thumbing through videos on YouTube about the new *Star Trek* series, wondering how badly they were going to screw it up this time. As I watched, I started feeling sick, experiencing the same sensations as when I'm about to have a migraine, which have plagued me all my life. A few seconds later, I started vomiting in the kitchen sink. This had never happened before. Walking back to my chair, I turned around to sit, and the next thing I remember is the very frightened face of my wife hovering over me, her voice urgently speaking to me. To this day, I cannot remember a word she said.

I was having a seizure.

Lynn came into the kitchen and found me rigid as a board,

slipping out of my chair, violently convulsing—with a towel stuffed in my mouth. Apparently, I realized I might bite my tongue off in the process of whatever was happening and took measures to prevent self-harm. She kept asking whether I was okay, then realized I was not. Something was dreadfully wrong. Grabbing me by the arms, my wife tried to keep me from hitting my head on the table, asking me if she should call 911. She pleaded with me to speak to her.

I have no memory of any of this.

I remember being sucked into a very dark, scary place and then—nothing. Just a gaping void in my memory. I don't remember becoming conscious again.

The next memory I have is sitting on the sofa with my wife next to me, stroking my arm, looking concerned. According to Lynn, I came out of the seizure and seemed to be conscious enough of what was happening around me. She asked whether I was okay, and I told her I was. When she asked whether I wanted to go sit in the living room on the sofa, I got up and almost fell face forward on the kitchen floor, so she helped usher me into the living room.

After a period of time sitting on the sofa, I was able to tell her who I was, what our address was, what the date was, and even who the president was. According to her recollection, I was making jokes. I remember none of this, but I can recall what happened afterward in bits and pieces. We discussed whether I should go to the emergency room. We googled "seizures" (okay, *Lynn* googled seizures; I was not capable of googling anything). We ultimately decided we would wait; if I had another, she would call 911 immediately. For now, though, I was going to rest, and she would keep a careful eye on me.

The next few days were painful. Because of all the convulsing, I had torn my biceps tendon in my shoulder, where I'd had previous surgeries. My back hurt, my hip hurt, and my head hurt. I had terrible headaches and felt miserable. My body was overcome with a feeling of being drained, as if I had just run a marathon. The whole episode had depressed me. It was more than a little scary, because I realized that at some point during that experience, I had felt as though I was dying. And in that brush with my own mortality, I understood once again:

I do not want to die, I want to live.

Why We Must Keep Changing

Over the past two years of working on this book, the entire world has undergone a massive shift, experiencing a global pandemic that changed the way people lived their lives. In many ways, this change caused me to shrink into a smaller life and use it as an excuse for receding from the lives of others. We were social distancing, right? We were wearing masks. That meant nobody had to see how bad my tremors had become. Nobody had to see how I often can't walk throughout the day, how much I was degenerating. Nobody had to see how my jaw and lip quiver now, uncontrollably—how my body is, in many ways, detached from my brain. When the tremors got to be their worst, nobody had to see me when the meds were wearing off. When I had the apathetic frozen mask of a Parkinson's patient, I could exist without having to be ashamed of how sick I'd become.

I started this book with the admonition that you must read this or die, period. In the past, I would have wanted to write something that demonstrated how I had faced a challenge, discovered a way to overcome it, and succeeded in that pursuit. Then I would show you how to do the same. While that can happen, it's not really how life works. We're all going to die—whether you read this book or not.

The only difference between you and me is perhaps I'm a little more aware of that fact. I have no way of knowing what your experience is, but I do know that life eventually ends, and no matter what kind of answer, solution, thinking, or exercise I give you, I can't prevent that from happening to you—or me.

If we are fortunate, we are all going to become old enough to see our physical vigor diminish and struggle with the frustration of a gradually waning mental acuity. That's the course of all life: we start out weak and fragile, make something of ourselves, and end the same way we came into this world—that is, vulnerable. It's the way of all flesh. When I was facing death once again, I had the opportunity to consider why I felt shame about my disease and what was so scary about death. Part of it was some unfinished business. There are things I want to do, money I want to set aside for my family, a few more accomplishments I want to check off the old bucket list. Mostly, though, I don't want to leave anyone with unnecessary burdens, but that's not really up to me. It's a noble idea, of course, but none of us gets to decide when and how we leave this life. Although part of me would like to live a very long time, that is unlikely. I've come to realize that staying alive is not the same as living.

A deep part of my will to live, I'm sure, is a basic survival instinct, shared by any organism doing what it's designed to do. But it feels like more than that. This thing I call *me*—the spirit, the soul, the mind—wanted to keep going, even when I was lying on the ground, convulsing. As horrible and agonizing as the experience of living can be, I prefer it to the alternative. I'll never forget the look of fear on my wife's face as I came out of the seizure; I realized that when I exit this stage of being, it's going to hurt more people than just me. In fact, my pain will come to an end, but the pain of those around me will continue until their stories conclude.

Our lives are not just our own; our stories are inextricably woven in the fabric of others' lives.

The choice to fully embrace life goes beyond merely not dying. Just existing is not enough—I have to keep living. And as we all shed our masks and slowly venture back into the world, I have no excuse not to be present, not to show up the way I am, no matter the consequences. This is the choice to live, to not only endure but bring all of who you are, whatever that means, to each and every day for as long as you can.

Showing Up as You Are

Recently, I attended a video call with some of my closest friends and confidants, a mastermind group I've been a part of for many years. This group of entrepreneurs has met for nearly a decade, sharing the ups and downs in our personal and professional journeys. The week following my seizure and slow recovery it was my turn to sit in the "hot seat" and share a question or problem with the group. "I think I'd like to just share what happened to me," I said, "if that's all right with everyone."

For the next hour I told my story, sharing much of what I've written here. That group of ambitious professionals watched and listened, and as I concluded, it occurred to me I hadn't felt that supported in years—because I had allowed myself to be seen. By inviting others into part of my story, allowing them to accept or reject me, I felt more connected to other human beings and more human myself.

That, my friend, is living: to show up just the way you are and be okay with whatever happens next. To let yourself quake and tremor, to invite even the most embarrassing parts of yourself to the conversation of life, without hiding anything. I don't have many wise words these days, and I'm not quite sure where my health will be even six months from now, let alone in a year. But I do know what it means to live and why it's important to keep showing up as long as I can, however I can, doing my best to demonstrate to others how important it is to live while we're still alive.

And so, at the risk of sounding like a Hallmark card, all we have is this moment. Today. And what's important is what we do with it, that we live as fully as we can, whether we are underneath the wings of a hang glider, climbing a rock wall, or riding around in a wheelchair. My goal these days is to embrace life for what it is: a strange and seemingly unlikely occurrence, a bizarre but exciting and mostly enjoyable experience that can also scare the crap out of you.

In most situations, we have a certain amount of choice regarding how we process our experiences, even the hard ones. We can decide to imbue these moments with meaning, or we can despair about the potential pointlessness of it all. We can look for what's good, noble, and pure, choosing to be okay during the times when we would rather say, "This is a load of shit." That's living: not denying the harshness of reality but finding a way to move through another day in spite of the difficulties we all face. To live is to bravely face the darkness yet again and not be consumed by it.

You may be wondering where I stand now as to what I believe and the foundations upon which I base my life. In regard to Parkinson's, I wish it hadn't been dumped on me. But at the same time, I recognize the gift it provided: a true lust for life. In spite of the difficult circumstances the disease brought, it has taught me a valuable lesson. The situation is what it is. And yet, I prefer this experience to the blackness of the void; that is, to not being. And whether I'm destined for a quickly degenerative condition that takes me deeper into the abyss or to the streets of heaven, the point is to recognize that all I have is what's right in front of me. That means making the decision to keep living for as long as I can, rather than dying before they put me in the grave.

As a friend recently reminded me, this is what it meant when Jesus said the kingdom of God is here and now. Life is to be experienced—not in resisting what is or denying the truth that stands in front of you, but in embracing all of existence. So while you're here, if I may, try to *live as much as you can.*

Through this book, I've taken you on the journey I experienced, and like the snake swallowing its own tail, you could say we've come full circle. My quest began by stepping deeply into doubt, agnosticism, atheism, even nihilism. I floundered and prospered there for a while, gleaning what I could from each of those beliefs and carrying their lessons with me. I have, as the Israelites did, spent my own time wandering in the wilderness and come out in a land unlike the one I inhabited before.

It's worth noting that I put my faith back in God, but in a very different way.

These days, I'm comfortable with the unknown. I am more likely to trust what I call God without understanding why or how, and I am less likely to make definitive statements about how "He" works. Faith, like the science of neural pathways, is more of a mystery than we pretend to believe, and I'm okay with that. I actually find it comforting. To trust in what we cannot see amid an incredibly confounding existence, in its own way, makes great sense. I've reached a point, finally, where I can hold the known and unknowable with both outstretched hands, ready to receive whatever is next.

This is my life now: fewer answers, greater trust. I don't know what tomorrow will bring. I don't know whether my brain will ever heal, when I might die, or how much of my faculties I will have left when I do. I don't know whether I'll achieve everything I want to do in this life. And that's okay. I don't need to know that. "Consider the lilies of the field, how they grow: they neither toil nor spin . . ." And that is just what I will do.

While the flowers grow and the birds sing, and the world keeps turning, I will try to pay attention to it all. I will try to experience as much as I can with as little worry as possible, to truly enjoy life, to marvel at the sheer mathematical insanity of my being here. I will *try* to not worry about what comes next and choose today to live. And with all my heart, I wish you the same.

DO THIS

Do something. Try something you've never tried before. Reach out to a friend or loved one and tell them what you're struggling with. Share with someone what's going on with you, what you wish were different. You don't have to do this alone. We are all in this together. I hope to see you somewhere along the journey.

Acknowledgments

So many people in my life contributed to this book, and I have undoubtedly failed to include everyone here who deserves recognition. Please know the omission is unintentional.

First, for believing in me and the message of this book enough to encourage me to write it—and then to collaborate with me—I am grateful to Jeff Goins. Every word on every page is better because of him.

My heartfelt gratitude to my wife, Lynn, and my son, Sean.

Love and respect to the men in the Green Room Mastermind, whom I have met with every week for the last decade: Mike Stelzner, Pat Flynn, Mark Mason, Cliff Ravenscraft, and Leslie Samuel.

Jon Acuff, thanks for teaching me so much (including the fact that my life is dope and I get to do dope stuff).

Deep respect and love for the Ray Edwards Company Team. You all make the work I do possible, and you make it (and me) better.

Acknowledgments

- Tami Hyatt, you've always had my back, and your loyalty is above reproach.

- Jenny Kerns, you are a never-ending source of love and joy.

- Bryan and Noelle Switalski, I feel so fortunate to work with such skilled agents of influence—thank you!

- Aida Jažić, thank you for your unfailing support, coaching, and encouragement over the last few years.

- Joe Pomeroy, you're a disciplined and faithful companion and co-worker.

- Juan Lopez, you make us look great—literally.

- Kris Edwards, my brother, working with you is a dream come true. You amaze me with your creativity and willingness to "go the extra mile."

Thanks also to Pete Vargas, Michael Hyatt, Gail Hyatt, Mike Kim, Megan Hyatt-Miller, Brian Dixon, Joel Miller, Mary Hyatt, Carrie Wilkerson, David Hancock, Jim and Chris Howard, Jennifer Allwood, Martin Howey, Frank Kern, Jim Rutz, Ben Settle, Kary Oberbrunner, Ed Hill, James Wedmore, Chris Ducker, Phil Mershon, Sean Cannell, Paul B. Evans, Joel Comm, Chad Allen, Jeff Walker, Jon Walker, Diane Walker, Donald and Betsy Miller, Dr. J. J. Peterson, Paul and Melissa Pruett, April Sunshine, Ben Greenfield, Amy Porterfield, Stu McLaren, Chalene Johnson, Brian Kurtz, Perry Marshall, Pedro Adao, Frank Viola, Dan Miller, Chad Cannon, Armand Morin, and Alex Mandossian.

To my readers, podcast listeners, clients, and customers, thank you for letting me serve you and for your constant feedback and support.

References for Deeper Reading

Instead of a dry list of references, I thought I'd share a list of the books I read that influenced this work, as well as some additional resources for further exploration for those interested in the topics covered in this book. I'll share them below in a brief bibliographic essay. And if you want more, please feel free to email me at ray@rayedwards.com.

Introduction· Saved by a Sales Letter

The original "Read This Or Die" title came from a Jim Rutz letter he wrote to help sell magazines for people wanting to get healthier. If you want to read the original letter, you can google his name and the title of that letter to find a number of websites republishing it.

The Abraham Maslow reference about no more than 1 to 2 percent of the population actualizing their potential may, in fact, be apocryphal. However, you can find a number of researchers quoting him, saying at most only two out of one hundred people achieve what they're truly capable of. Although I could not identify the origin of the quote, I chose to keep it in the book, because it rang true and there were others who seemed to support it.

I mentioned a personal story about a conversation I had with Frank Kern. Frank is a living legend in the world of direct-response copywriting, and if the subject matter of this book intrigues you, I would highly recommend checking out his website: frankkern.com.

The basic structure for this book was informed by my own approach to copywriting that I've refined over the years, what I call the PASTOR framework for writing sales pages. You can learn more about it, as well as the work that I do, at rayedwards.com.

Part I· Pain—Start with What Hurts

In the opening section to part I, I quoted Robert Collier, who wrote that you should always enter the conversation that's already happening in the customer's mind. Collier essentially invented copywriting in the 1930s, and although he died in 1950, he is still a well-respected member of our community. I could not locate the specific origin of this quote, but all his work is worth reading, and I highly recommend it. He is a delightfully weird guy and makes for some enjoyable reading, depending on how seriously you want to take him. All his stuff on copywriting is solid—especially *The Robert Collier Letter Book* (New York: McGraw-Hill, 1931), but I especially enjoy *The Book of Life* (New York: Collier, 1925), which was later retitled and repackaged as *Secret of the Ages* (New York: Collier, 1926). Both these titles will serve you well.

Chapter 1: Letting Go of Lies We Love

In chapter 1, I quoted Byron Katie, who likes to say that whenever she resists reality, it only wins every time. She says this in almost every book and talk she's ever given, but the best place to start with her work would be *Loving What Is* (New York: Harmony Books, 2002), which is easy to read but even better to listen to.

The Nietzsche "abyss" quote is one of my favorites and comes from his seminal work *Beyond Good and Evil* (1886; New York: Penguin, 2003). The full quote is: "Battle not with monsters, lest ye become a monster, and if you gaze into the abyss, the abyss gazes also into you." I love this quote, because it speaks to the journey of existential confusion I went through and that I think a lot of people experience. If you are going to question the very nature of reality, be aware of the fire you are playing with. Tread lightly. This isn't kid stuff and can take you to some dark places if you are not careful (and even sometimes when you are).

Chapter 2: Facing Reality

The quote by Frederick Buechner about "beautiful and terrible things" happening in the world comes from his devotional book *Beyond Words: Daily Readings in the ABCs of Faith* (San Francisco: HarperOne, 2004). A longer version of the quote is: "Here is your life. You might never have been, but you *are*, because the party wouldn't have been complete without you. Here is the world. Beautiful and terrible things will happen. Don't be afraid." Buechner is a deep well of inspiration, and you would be wise to read anything by him, especially *The Sacred Journey* (San Francisco: Harper & Row, 1982), which is a short memoir of the first half of his life.

The Richard Feynman "first principle" quote comes from a commencement speech he delivered on June 14, 1974, to the graduating class of the California Institute of Technology. In context, the quote is:

"The first principle is that you must not fool yourself—and you are the easiest person to fool. So you have to be very careful about that. After you've not fooled yourself, it's easy not to fool other scientists. You just have to be honest in a conventional way after that." You can google "Cargo-Cult Science speech" and find a copy of the speech online.

Chapter 3: Beliefs Are Engines for Change
The reference to Thomas Merton wanting someone to thank may be apocryphal. I first heard mention of it from Parker J. Palmer, who wrote about Merton in his book *Let Your Life Speak* (San Francisco: Jossey-Bass, 2000). Merton had a longtime affinity for and curiosity about Buddhism, having spent significant time with Zen monks toward the end of his life, drawing parallels between their practices and those of his own monastic order. If you've never read *Seeds of Contemplation* (Norfolk, CT: New Directions, 1949), that's a good place to start with Merton. He does a great job of walking the line between traditional religion and a more mystical approach to life. At times when fundamentalism wears me down, I find his work reinvigorating.

The Viktor Frankl quote about everything being taken from us but our ability to choose comes from the classic *Man's Search for Meaning* (Boston: Beacon Press, 1963). In addition to being one of the bestselling books of the twentieth century, it's also easy to read and hard to put down. That book is a treasure trove of meaning. I highly recommend it for anyone trying to find a deeper purpose in life.

Part II· Amplify—It Gets Worse Before It Gets Better

Chapter 4: Turn Up the Volume
The reference to Nir Eyal's work and why our brains are neurolog-

ically wired to avoid pain "all the way down" comes from his book *Indistractable* (Dallas: Ben Bella Books, 2019), which is an eye-opening account of how our brains work in this age of increasing distractions.

Influence by Robert Cialdini (New York: Harper Business, 2021) is, of course, a classic and the source of my quote of him in this chapter.

The Nietzsche quote about "he who has a why can bear almost any how" may be apocryphal as I couldn't find the original source, but it is so compelling and such a part of the cultural conversation around meaning that I have chosen to leave it. If you've never read any Nietzsche other than the occasional online quote, I'd recommend giving him a try. There's a reason people are still quoting him today. You may not agree with everything he says, but his mind was nonetheless brilliant. For my money, I'd start with *Thus Spake Zarathustra* (1883; New York: Penguin, 1961).

The Earl Nightingale reference that "we become what we think about" is a quote from his classic self-help audio program called "The Strangest Secret." The whole thing is less than thirty minutes long, and you can find free versions of it on YouTube. This is one of my favorite old-school self-help programs. I still listen to it when I need a boost of motivation.

Chapter 5: People Change When They Have To, Not When They Want To

All references to est and Sheridan Fenwick's exploration of their methodologies comes from her book *Getting It: The Psychology of est* (New York: Penguin, 1977; particularly pages 122–23). I recommend reading this fascinating book to understand how modern-day religious cults and self-help movements are still orchestrated. It's all the same playbook and fascinating to observe once you know the patterns.

Carmen Paglia wrote a paper on "Cults and Consciousness" that you can find online with a quick search.

Part III· Story—Believing in a Better Future

Chapter 7: When Old Stories No Longer Serve Us

To learn more about the work of Hale Dwoskin and the Sedona Method, check out sedona.com or pick up his book *The Sedona Method* (Sedona, AZ: Sedona Press, 2003). Both my wife and I have gone through this training and found it life changing and paradigm shifting.

Principia Discordia, written by Greg Hill with Kerry Wendell Thornley and others (Port Townsend, WA: Loompanics, 1979; 5th edition), is a weird little book from the counterculture movement in the 1970s. The whole "all statements are true" quote was a quirky way to share my own eclectic range of influences. If you want to be reminded of how hippies used to express themselves (or be introduced to it for the first time), you can easily order the book online, which was originally published anonymously. Fair warning, though: it doesn't make much sense. And that's the point.

Part IV· Testimony—Evidence Worth Believing

Chapter 9: Reinforcing New Realities

The references to Tim Ferriss and the ketogenic diet come from Tim's book *The 4-Hour Body: An Uncommon Guide to Rapid Fat Loss, Incredible Sex, and Becoming Superhuman* (New York: Harmony, 2010) and his podcast, *The Tim Ferriss Show*. To learn more about this approach to eating and diet, you can search his website at tim.blog or pick up the book (which is better in print than via digital copy).

To learn more about the philosophy of Ayn Rand and the collection of essays I quoted—*Philosophy: Who Needs It?* (New York: Signet, 1984)—you can visit her website aynrand.org. The book can be found at most booksellers. And if you're looking for some thoughtful fiction, I recommend picking up *The Fountainhead* (Indianapolis: Bobbs Merril, 1943).

The references to Joe Dispenza come from his books *Breaking the Habit of Being Yourself* (Carlsbad, CA: Hay House, 2012) and *You Are the Placebo* (Carlsbad, CA: Hay House, 2014). Dispenza's work has had a massive impact on my life, health, and worldview. He can sound a little "woo" at first, but I have found his insights and experiments to be fascinating and often refreshing. *Breaking the Habit* is probably an easier introduction to him and his work, though. You can also learn more about him at drjoedispenza.com.

The quote by Ralph Waldo Emerson comes from his short but powerful essay "Self-Reliance," which was first published in 1841. Emerson was once a preacher, so all his essays tend to be structured as speeches (or perhaps more appropriately, sermons). This one in particular is full of punchy quotes and pithy takeaways. He may be the first writer of the "tweetable."

Part VI· Response—Making It Stick

Chapter 13: Imagine the Worst

Joe Rogan has said more than once on his podcast, *The Joe Rogan Experience*, that he thinks all religions are basically cults. But one specific reference comes from episode "#1055—Bret Weinstein," where he has a conversation with Bret Weinstein about the differences between a cult and a religion. He does, somewhat comically, call the Catholic Church a cult of a billion people and compares the pope to a wizard with a pointy hat. I admit that I laughed. You can find a lengthy excerpt of this interview on the JRE Clips YouTube channel. Or look up the original.

Chapter 14: Remove All Risk

Zig Ziglar is a legend in the world of self-help, and I grew up listening to him. The quote on climbing the ladder of success while dressed in the "costume of failure" is a powerful one that has never left my brain for long. This originally comes from his classic work *See You at the Top* (1975; Gretna, LA: Pelican Publishing, 2000). Pick it up if you get the chance; it still holds up.

Chapter 15: Commitment Has a Cost

Alex Hormozi's *$100M Offers: How to Make Offers So Good People Feel Stupid Saying No* (Carrollton, TX: Acquisition.com, 2021) is worth a read if you are in the business of selling anything—ideas, products, services, you name it—and have found that reason can only take you so far. Hormozi clearly demonstrates why and how logic doesn't hold a candle to psychology when it comes to persuasion. It's the feeling people want, not the reason behind it.